Intimacy and Power

Also by Derek Layder

STRUCTURE, INTERACTION AND SOCIAL THEORY

THE REALIST IMAGE IN SOCIAL SCIENCE

NEW STRATEGIES IN SOCIAL RESEARCH

UNDERSTANDING SOCIAL THEORY

METHODS, SEX AND MADNESS (*with J. O'Connell-Davidson*)

MODERN SOCIAL THEORY

SOCIOLOGICAL PRACTICE

SOCIAL AND PERSONAL IDENTITY

EMOTION IN SOCIAL LIFE

Intimacy and Power

The Dynamics of Personal Relationships in Modern Society

Derek Layder
University of Leicester, UK

First published 2009 by
PALGRAVE MACMILLAN

Palgrave Macmillan in the UK is an imprint of Macmillan Publishers Limited, registered in England, company number 785998, of Houndmills, Basingstoke, Hampshire RG21 6XS.

Palgrave Macmillan in the US is a division of St Martin's Press LLC, 175 Fifth Avenue, New York, NY 10010.

Palgrave Macmillan is the global academic imprint of the above companies and has companies and representatives throughout the world.

Palgrave® and Macmillan® are registered trademarks in the United States, the United Kingdom, Europe and other countries.

ISBN-13: 978–0–230–57956–9 hardback

This book is printed on paper suitable for recycling and made from fully managed and sustained forest sources. Logging, pulping and manufacturing processes are expected to conform to the environmental regulations of the country of origin.

A catalogue record for this book is available from the British Library.

A catalog record for this book is available from the Library of Congress.

10   9   8   7   6   5   4   3   2   1
18   17   16   15   14   13   12   11   10   09

Printed and bound in Great Britain by
CPI Antony Rowe, Chippenham and Eastbourne

Contents

Preface and Acknowledgements

This book is about the intimacy and power games that underpin personal relationships between couples (and, to a lesser extent, friends) in the modern world. It focuses primarily, but not exclusively, on the interpersonal dynamics of relationships between couples (and friends) by asking questions such as 'How is intimacy "achieved"? How do people make close relationships work? What happens when their intimacy stalls, or breaks down completely?' These are serious analytic questions for any science of human behaviour, but are infrequently broached by sociologists. Yet such questions are too important to be left entirely to self-help gurus and writers of popular psychology (which is not to deny the usefulness of some of their contributions).

For these and other reasons, this book concentrates on a fairly restricted band of interest in intimacy compared with the potential spread of sociological enquiry. In this respect it is not a critical overview of existing social research on the many different facets of intimacy. As I've already said, it mainly concerns intimacy in couples and friendship and, as such, it does not cover issues about parenting or parent–child interactions. Nor is it explicitly about the role of sexuality in intimacy – although obviously it is assumed that sexuality frequently plays a major role in couple intimacy in a way that it doesn't in friendships. Following from this, the book does not explore contrasts between heterosexual and same sex relationships. It is assumed that although there may be differences between them, they share much in common in terms of the human experience of intimacy.

Gender issues do figure quite prominently in the discussion. However, the main focus is on the debate about the extent to which differences in intimacy skills and the negotiation of intimate relationships result from gender influences. The question of gender roles (such as the persistence of notions of 'female housewives' versus 'male earners') within marriage or cohabitation, or the topic of gender inequalities and exploitation, is not explicitly examined. The main concerns are about how couples (and/or friends) communicate with each other in the context of different types of intimacy and the typical confusions, problems and conflicts that arise.

Intimacy involves personal closeness – both physical, and psycho-emotional – and in this sense, many aspects of human contact may be defined as intimate. Thus it is common to speak of having 'intimate conversations' or sharing intimate situations – even with people we might otherwise regard as strangers. Such interactions occur regularly in gym changing rooms, on aircraft, trains, buses, and in many public spaces. Now while it may be that a 'version' of 'intimacy' is shared in such instances, it is, nonetheless, usually fleeting and, as I say, often involves individuals who aren't particularly well known to each other. Both characteristics make this phenomenon very different from that which is the focus of this book. Here the concern is with intimate relationships sustained over time by deep mutual (psycho-emotional) knowledge.

'Self-disclosure' (Giddens 1992) and 'disclosing intimacy' (Jamieson 1998) are terms that have been used to characterise close relationships in the modern world. Unfortunately, these terms do not distinguish between perfunctory or superficial self-disclosure – of the kind frequently present in fleeting moments of 'intimacy' – and a more profound kind of self-revelation stemming from sustained contact, shared experience and deep mutual knowledge. Both for this reason and because (as I go on to show), the extent and form of self-disclosure in modern couple intimacy varies considerably, I prefer to talk of 'deep knowledge intimacy' rather than self-disclosure or disclosing intimacy.

Finally, there are many people – too numerous to mention – who have influenced my thinking on intimacy over the years and to whom I am grateful. More specifically, I would like to thank Barbara Misztal for her comments on earlier drafts of what now appear as parts of Chapters 1 and 12. Also, Nicky Drucquer provided a thorough and perceptive commentary on most of the chapters as they appeared in earlier forms. Her insightful comments helped me greatly in reformulating some of the ideas.

1
Understanding Couple Intimacy

Since its earliest beginnings a prominent theme in sociological analysis has been to document the cataclysmic social changes that have accompanied the transition from pre-modern (traditional) societies to their modern and late modern forms. A concern with the profound changes in social relationships that resulted from this transition is reflected in the work of the classical sociologists Comte, Durkheim, Marx, Weber and Simmel. Such an emphasis has also been present in the writings of subsequent authors such as Parsons and Elias. In a similar fashion, recent sociological works, particularly by Giddens (1991, 1992) and Beck and Beck-Gernsheim (1995), are themed around the issue of how intimacy has been changed by the structural transition to modernity. These authors have stressed the way in which traditional constraints and expectations have been stripped away to leave intimate relationships bereft of such external supports. They have identified the emergence of what they call 'the pure relationship', which has meant that intimate relationships have become increasingly fragile, as their external anchorages have fallen away.

I shall have reason to discuss the pure relationship at many points in this book. However, in so doing I shall be more concerned with the nature of the pure relationship and its implications for personal and social experience than with the question of how intimacy has changed from pre-modern to modern times. In particular, I focus on how the pure relationship measures up against what we know of the interpersonal dynamics of intimacy, as they are experienced in the modern world. This entails something of a shift of emphasis away from a concern with social structural matters – involved in the transition from traditional to modern societies – to a *relatively greater* concern with understanding intimacy as an interpersonal transaction.

However, in suggesting this, I am by no means advocating that interpersonal dynamics are the exclusive outcome of 'internal' situational factors. Of course, historical developments in social structure and culture are extremely important but these 'external' factors must be understood in combination with equally important subjective psychological factors, *as well as* the dynamics of socially situated behaviour. In this respect, what I call the theory of social domains (Layder 1997) furnishes the underlying explanatory framework of this study. While this remains largely in the background its influence is critical. More generally, however, intimacy cannot be properly understood without due attention to the interpersonal dealings and transactions which are, in fact, its primary means of expression. In short, the way people 'do', or 'enact', intimacy is of paramount importance to understanding its nature.

Variations in couple intimacy

Chapter 2 begins with an overview of Giddens' (1991, 1992) and Beck and Beck-Gernsheim's (1995) accounts of the emergence of the pure relationship in the modern era, but quickly moves on to a critical commentary on them. This critique draws from 'alternative' empirical data on couple relationships – reinforced by other critical voices – which suggest a somewhat different story about the nature of modern intimacy. The point is not to question the historical basis of Giddens' and Beck and Beck-Gernsheim's accounts of the transition from intimacy in traditional society to the modern pure relationship. However, a close examination of the empirical material reveals that the complex experiential character of modern couple intimacy differs from that suggested by the pure relationship.

Reibstein's (1997) study of protective dependent love, Marshall's (2006) research on the problems that couples have in sustaining optimal intimacy over the longer term, along with Miller's research on what he calls 'intimate terrorism', provide detailed and vivid evocations of these alternative visions of intimacy. Along with Jamieson's (1998, 1999) extensive review of work on different aspects of intimacy and Craib's (1998) critique of Giddens, the evidence suggests that modern couple intimacy is rather more complex, plural and nuanced than is suggested by the pure relationship. On this basis Chapter 2 goes on to outline six qualitatively different types of intimate relationship. In this sense, modern intimacy is to be understood not as a unitary 'pure relationship' but as a series of types whose characteristics may vary over time. The bundles of characteristics or dimensions that form these types include the extent and nature of self-disclosure between partners; varying forms of trust, commitment and satisfaction; communicative styles, the matching or mismatching of psycho-emotional needs, argumentative or conflict styles and so on. However, the most important variable characteristic is the form of interpersonal power and control underpinning the intimacy in question.

Intimate agendas and alignment

Individuals have different levels of personal and subjective power – as indicated by the existence of varying amounts of self-confidence, persuasive skills, capacity to get things done, or make a difference. Chapter 3 examines how these varying powers profoundly impact on couple's everyday negotiations about intimacy. Identifying the exact balance of power, control and influence underpinning a close relationship provides a clue as to what is going on in the minds of the intimates as they search for psychological and emotional satisfaction. In this respect a basic driving force in intimacy concerns the 'agendas' of the participants: what do they each want, desire or need from the bond? Do they simply want to feel included in the other's agenda or do they want to be part of a shared project? Do they wish to be regarded as a team, or simply want their thoughts or feelings to be acknowledged? Do they desire, or need, definite expressions of love or closeness – like hugs or kisses, or verbal statements of support or concern? Are they driven by the need to encourage one another and/or to disclose more about their desires and feelings?

Although partners and friends may share interests and attitudes, their respective psycho-biographical journeys generate differences in emotional sensitivities as well as practical needs. For example, they may have different requirements about personal space, how much love and affection they want, or how much they value the relationship. Even the extent of criticism and support they expect from one another may differ. Differences in need and disposition are potential sources of strain, tension or conflict. Personal agendas become the foci of 'negotiations' – either explicit or unconscious – which affect how partners 'get on' on a day-to-day basis. The way in which they deal with such negotiations will affect the closeness and robustness of their bond in the longer term.

Alignment between intimates is also important. Do their purposes and agendas mesh or conflict? Severe problems may result from mismatching agendas. There are three main possibilities. First, alignment problems may be situation-specific. For example, after dining out friends or partners may have a 'friendly' disagreement about who pays the bill. Second, interpersonal business may carry over from a previous encounter to influence alignment in the current situation. Continuing the example, whoever paid last time, and how everyone felt about it, in all likelihood will colour the emotional atmosphere of the next encounter. Finally, over long chains of encounters the general alignment of those involved will determine their ongoing moods and, as a consequence, how distant or close they become.

Interpersonal control and intimacy

Chapter 4 takes up the issue of interpersonal power, control and influence in intimacy. When circumstances permit, individuals try to minimise uncertainty and unpredictability in their relationships with others and this is linked to their ability to derive psycho-emotional benefits from intimate contact – such as support, approval, love, companionship, self-disclosure and so on. Emotions are the key to this process in which a relatively stable and well-adjusted sense of self-identity results from interpersonal negotiations of control and influence. Thus people are continually involved in power – in the positive sense of empowerment – through acts of personal mastery and what I call 'benign control', or mutually negotiated relations of control and influence that meet the needs of all those involved and which minimise manipulation based on self-interest.

Since intimacy requires psychological and physical closeness, mutual benign forms of power and control are most relevant to its success. But it is mistaken to think of mutually satisfying intimacy as totally pure, unsullied by elements of selfishness or milder forms of manipulation. In this sense, 'softer' persuasive and manipulative control often plays a central role. Only when there is excessive disregard for the rights, needs and desires of another in a personal relationship, does control and influence become more manipulative and exploitative – as in instances of emotional blackmail or psychological bullying. Three of the six types outlined in Chapter 2 represent intimate relationships based on mutual benign, or benign-manipulative, control. The other three are more closely linked with manipulation exploitation. But all six are closely related in the sense that they often contain elements or mixtures of elements from each other. While mutually satisfying intimacy will, from time to time, contain manipulative or oppressive elements, the more exploitative types may occasionally be punctuated by brief or perfunctory gestures of care or affection.

In this regard some kinds of manipulation, oppressiveness or pretence are more or less socially acceptable than others. They do not, in every case, refer to situations in which people are duped or coerced. Perhaps more disturbingly, partners or friends often freely accept some level of manipulation, oppressiveness or pretence as 'normal' or acceptable. Of course, mutually satisfying intimate relationships rely on open communication and fluid alterations of power. But the *sine qua non* of optimal intimacy is that no one person dominates the relationship over time. If power positions become rigidly entrenched, then lines of communication also begin to close down and intimacy rapidly deteriorates.

Intimacy skills, clashing styles and arguments

Chapter 5 focuses on the notion of intimacy as an art requiring particular skills such as being able to communicate affection or care, being able to talk about sensitive emotional issues (say, insecurities or desires) and being able to empathise. The more skilled a person is in the arts of intimacy, the more this contributes to her or his subjective powers – by boosting or depleting confidence, energy and enthusiasm. It is clear that some individuals are more skilled at intimacy than others. But, it is far more contentious to claim that differences in intimacy skills can be predicted by gender (Cameron 2007). In this regard enduring popular stereotypes suggesting that women are more accomplished than men in the interpersonal skills required for intimacy are reinforced by studies based on the assumption that there are 'fundamental' or 'essential' differences between men's and women's conversational styles and ways of relating (Gray 1992, Tannen 1992, 2002; Baron-Cohen 2004).

However, as Cameron points out, while there is scant evidence to support these claims, there is plenty of other evidence to suggest alternative, more complex explanations. The social domains perspective that frames this current study supports the main thrust of Cameron's argument, but takes it into new theoretical territory. Thus, Chapter 5 evaluates claims about gender differences in intimacy skills (such as the evidence for, and purpose of, cooperative – or 'rapport talk' – or of empathetic skills in men and women). However, the evaluation is made in the light of the influence of multiple social domains on social behaviour, and the way in which different forms of power and control play a leading role in the interpersonal dynamics of intimacy.

Chapter 6 turns the spotlight on other issues related to differences in intimacy skills. In particular, it asks questions about whether individual differences in style of communication have implications for attitudes towards self-disclosure and thus for the quality of intimacy or the fate of relationships. Conflict styles and the arguments they facilitate are also crucially important in influencing how partners get on with one another on a day-to-day basis. However, the main focus of Chapter 6 concerns the distinction between direct and indirect forms of communication and the effects that clashing individual styles have on couple's feelings and emotions. It is important to distinguish between different forms of indirectness in the expression of emotion in order to tease out their implications for intimacy. In this respect personal control and emotional blocking are of pivotal importance.

Intimacy strategies: Personal repertoires

Given that couples pursue agendas formed around their emotional and psychological needs, the question of *how* they pursue them becomes crucial, and this is the focus of Chapter 7. Each person tends to employ her or his own favoured methods and means of achieving what they want or need. Such strategies, ploys and skills are part of a personal repertoire of control manoeuvres and may be in the service of benign or exploitative motives – and the positive and negative emotions that go along with them. The emotional architecture that underpins self-identities plays a large part in shaping personal repertoires of interpersonal control and influence. In a sense a person's preferred strategies and ploys will be directly related to her or his psycho-emotional agenda within the relationship – what they want, need or desire from intimate partners. But intimate relationships also require joint emotion work in order to preserve their integrity.

   As for specific strategies, ploys or manoeuvres, there is a considerable range of possibilities depending on whether the relationship is mutually satisfying or in serious decline. Mutually satisfying relationships can be expected to include various forms of (psychological) seduction and persuasion, enrolment, deals and pacts and so on, as well as 'inverted' manipulation – like giving away power and emotionally 'rescuing' a partner. At the other end of the scale, strategies include exploitative manipulation such as emotional blackmail or psychological terrorism.

Games, erosion and plurality in modern intimacy

In Chapters 8 and 9, I describe some typical energising and energy-draining power and control games to be found in committed relationships. This extends the analysis of personal strategies, tactics and ploys to more complex 'patterns of relating' that develop over the longer term. Intimacy 'games' emerge from the combined interplay of individual behaviour, personal relationships and chains of everyday encounters (Collins 2005). In pursuing their respective agendas, purposes and strategies, intimates either support and enhance, or diminish and undermine one another's self-esteem and self-confidence. 'Energy-draining' games channel physical and emotional energy away from a relationship through the absence of loving gestures or support, or by deliberate efforts of partners to wound or attack one another. Energising games work on the reverse principle. Through care, support and loving gestures, individuals and relationships are energised precisely because intimates confirm or boost one another's self-confidence, self-esteem and approval.

Mutually satisfying intimacy rests on a delicate balance of an array of tensions and forces such as that between individuality (personal space) and the need for togetherness. The continuous shifting of the focus and balance of power is also integral to optimal intimacy because it allows partners to genuinely share in setting the direction and tone of the relationship. Permanent or complete equality does not exist in such a relationship. The survival of mutually satisfying intimacy rests on the continual rotation of power and control in tandem with open dialogue. Partners take the lead on a broadly equitable basis. But even the best of personal relationships never reach an ideal or 'pure' state. Mutually satisfying intimacy is always a 'work in progress'. Even the most sort-after intimacy – what I call 'dynamic intimacy' – rests on an ever-changing (and thus inherently) fragile balance.

Chapter 10 confronts the fact of the fragility of modern intimacy by examining how it rapidly degrades when its interpersonal supports are removed, accidentally damaged, or fall away as the result of neglect. The chapter is driven by the question of why it is that a great many relationships that were once mutually satisfying, while not being destroyed completely, slowly but surely deteriorate, becoming flat and de-energised. It examines some of the key interpersonal dynamics that underlie the process of erosion and the unravelling of energising intimacy games. Particularly important is the problem of emotional blocking first raised in Chapter 6. A continuous cycle of emotional blocking reinforces the conflicts and arguments generated by communication problems between partners. Also crucial are problems of habituation and the emotional estrangement it may cause.

Chapter 11 brings the different strands of the discussion together in terms of a critical dialogue with the notion of the pure relationship. The evidence and arguments offered in this book amply demonstrate

that modern intimacy is multidimensional. There are significant variations in communication and self-disclosure and the quality and nature
of trust, commitment and satisfaction in close relationships. Although
it is undoubtedly true that modern intimacy is fragile, the reasons for
its fragility are not necessarily those that the proponents of the pure
relationship suggest. In this regard the important role of interpersonal
power and control is vastly underplayed, if not overlooked entirely. In
short, modern intimacy is plural, complex and nuanced in ways not
envisaged by the pure relationship.

Chapter 12 pursues these questions further in relation to more general
issues in social theory. First, the analysis of intimacy presented in this
book relies on the theory of social domains with its multidimensional
view of power. This provides a central vantage from which to critically evaluate some of Goffman's, Giddens' and Collins' views on the
nature of interpersonal relations, human subjectivity and their relation
to structural and institutional phenomena. Some of the inadequacies
of these views stem from an inability to embrace a multidimensional
view of power and to acknowledge the relatively independent properties of social domains. Finally, the chapter traces some of these more
general theoretical ideas and concepts and their implications for the
pure relationship.

Modern intimacy: A many splendoured thing

Giddens suggests that 'mutual disclosure' is central to modern intimacy
and while he has a point, he also overstates the case. Undoubtedly,
there has been an intensification of mutual disclosure and an increasing recognition of its importance. However, the distinctive feature of
modern intimacy is not mutual disclosure *per se*, but the various forms
it may take. Disclosure comes in varying forms and degrees, depending on the needs of the intimates and how their relationship plays out,
emotionally and practically. The same is true of trust and commitment.
Varying standards of mutual satisfaction, communication, disclosure,
trust and commitment emerge from the ever-present flow of negotiation
and 'emotion work' in intimacy. Just as there is no single type of intimacy, so there are no uniform versions of trust and commitment. In this
respect I have to agree with Jamieson (1998) that modern intimacy is
multidimensional – it is various and many-sided. While Jamieson tends
to focus on variations in intimacy deriving from structural influences,
this study concentrates on the crucial importance of interpersonal factors. The social domains view of intimacy not only suggests variation in

types of intimacy, but also suggests variation in underpinning forms of power and control. Even the most 'balanced' relationships are based on shifting patterns of power and control.

Mutual benign control enables couples (or friends) to obtain what they need and desire from one another in the way of love, approval, validation, companionship and so on. Crucially, however, it not only involves taking control, but also involves swapping, and relinquishing it at different times. The very close link between benign control and more manipulative and coercive forms is also of great importance. That these two seemingly opposite types of power and control can so easily slip, or morph into each other, is the underlying reason why personal relationships are so various. Intimacy cannot be measured only by its 'optimal' manifestations even though these may be its most sort-after, or socially acceptable. Benign and exploitative intimacy are two sides of the same coin, they are mirror images that exist – to differing extents – in all its forms. Thus, in this sense, to speak of 'pure' relationships is rather misleading.

Control in personal relationships ranges from benign, seductive and persuasive influence, through the manipulation of emotional blackmail and ending up with the extremes of emotional terrorism, bullying and physical coercion. Although routine intimacy games and relationship habits are similarly divided between benign and exploitative types, they are also closely related. Thus there are mutually satisfying, energising intimacy games as well as energy-draining ones, more closely resembling war zones. But again, they are never simply pure types. They contain diverse elements – bits and pieces – of others, lumped together in a unique amalgam.

The mixture of benign and exploitative, satisfying and unsatisfying intimacy speaks to the fact that close relationships are frequently sullied by jealousy, disappointment, even despair (Craib 1998). Problems are intrinsic to personal relationships. Sometimes they appear right from the start, but in the main they emerge *after* the first exciting frissons of 'getting to know one other' have worn off. Only when the routine aspects of day-to-day life are under way, are personalities and relationship compatibilities really tested. In long-term relationships, 'habituation' – especially as it concerns problems around taking one another for granted – is perhaps the greatest enemy of intimacy. Such problems tax to the full the ingenuity of partners or friends as they try to keep their enthusiasm for, and commitment to, one another alive and fresh.

2
The Varieties of Couple Intimacy

Modern intimacy is varied and plural rather than uniform and standardised as implied in the notion of the pure relationship. This complex and multidimensional view is supported by evidence from a number of research studies offering 'alternative' accounts of the nature of modern intimacy (Reibstein 1997, Marshall 2006, Miller 1995). The six types of intimate relationship identified later in the chapter are consistent with both the primary data from these studies (based on hundreds of hours of interviews and structured conversations with couples) and the secondary analysis of countless other empirically based studies (see Jamieson 1998 for an overview of such studies). A critical evaluation of these alternative accounts, and the evidence on which they are based, suggests that contemporary intimacy can be best understood in relation to a varied spectrum of types of personal relationship routinely found in couples and friends.

The emergence of the pure relationship

Both Giddens (1991, 1992) and Beck and Beck-Gernsheim (1995 – originally published in German in 1990) have developed accounts of the emergence of 'the pure relationship' in the modern era. They claim that this type of relationship has come to characterise intimate relationships as societies have moved away from pre-modern or traditional forms in which intimacy was governed by external criteria and the fixed rules and values enshrined in tradition. For example, marriage was the result of parental arrangement in order to cement an economic or political alliance, while 'friendship' hardly existed as a personal tie distinct from family membership. With the advent of the Western world changes in social structure have brought about a process of individualisation whereby people have become progressively freed from the restraints and constraints of traditional precepts and certainties, external control and moral laws, like those of religion and social class. In this respect personal biographies are now shaped by individual decisions and initiative. Family, marriage, parenthood, love and sexuality are no longer defined in a standard fashion; they 'vary in substance, expectations, norms and morality from individual to individual and from relationship to relationship'. Love itself becomes 'a blank that lovers must fill in themselves' (Beck and Beck-Gernsheim 1995: 5). In the form of the pure relationship love has replaced religion and social class in so far as it 'gives life purpose and meaning' (1995: 182), and has become something akin to a 'latter day secular religion' (1995: 175).

Giddens suggests that the pure relationship 'exists solely for whatever rewards that relationship can deliver' (1991: 6). A pure relationship 'is where a social relation is entered into for its own sake' and 'is continued only so far as it is thought by both parties to deliver enough satisfaction for each individual to stay within it' (1992: 58). Marriage or cohabitation has become a contract between two equal persons who expect to be emotionally and sexually satisfied by the relationship or they may leave and start another relationship with someone else. Friendship in modernity has likewise become a distinctive form of personal relationship entered into for its own sake. If the friends find they no longer gain mutual benefit from their bond then it may fall into disuse or be broken off.

Beck and Beck-Gernsheim emphasise the importance of labour market influences on the process of individualisation. Men and women are released from gender roles but at the same time are forced to build a life of their own in line with the imperatives of the labour market – such as training offers, social welfare regulations and benefits and job mobility. An individual's biography is planned around the requirements of the job market.

The fact that increasingly both partners are pursuing their own labour market biographies (because of women's greater participation in the labour force) comes into conflict with the demands of relationships and this causes the 'chaos of love' that characterises modern intimacy. The freeing up from tradition and external control requires that intimate relationships are conducted and expressed in terms of partner's (or friend's) own rules and decision-making which, as a consequence, makes them increasingly fragile. At the same time, the fragility of intimacy is further compounded by the difficulties created by the pursuance of two distinct labour market biographies (rather than meshing one labour market biography with a 'life-long housework biography' [1995: 6]).

In the pure relationship, says Giddens, 'trust can be mobilised only by a process of mutual disclosure' (1991: 6). Jamieson (1998) calls this 'disclosing intimacy' where thoughts and feelings are constantly revealed to one another. This is, in effect, a disclosure of the self – a phenomenon tied to what Giddens calls the reflexive project of the self. Disclosure of this type can lead to strong relations of trust and commitment which play a huge psychological role in cementing close bonds in the absence of external criteria (fixed, traditional rules and values). What keeps a pure relationship together is a freely given psychological and emotional investment in one another – as reflected in high levels of commitment and trust.

It is entirely up to the intimates themselves how they set the terms of their relationship and what rules and standards they apply to their conduct towards each other. The modern era is unique in so far as intimate relationships are created and renegotiated every day 'and not bound to fixed normative and value systems' (Kaspersen 2000: 107). Another feature of pure relationships particularly in couples is what Giddens calls 'plastic sexuality'. This refers to 'recreational' sexuality freed from the constraints of reproduction and which may become part of an individual's lifestyle and/'or a process of self-realisation'. As a vitally personal expression of the depth (or otherwise) of mutual feelings such sexuality is likely (though not necessarily) to be involved in the ongoing recreation and renegotiation of commitment and the expression of emotional satisfaction.

In this account of the pure relationship the emphasis is on the sociological problem of the nature of the transition from traditional to modern societies and the social processes and changes implicated in it. In this sense the type of intimacy defined by the pure relationship is thought to be a by-product of this transition. Clearly, this is a legitimate and important sociological problem. However, making the contrast between tradition and modernity the focus of analytic interest in intimacy necessitates a trade-off in terms of explanatory adequacy. It forces the analysis into very broad-brush characterisations of the changes involved in personal relationships. By compressing these changes under the single rubric of 'the pure relationship', much of the subtlety and complexity of modern intimacy, as it is lived and experienced by real couples and friends, is overlooked.

The upshot of this is that elements of intimacy such as trust, commitment and disclosure are viewed in a rather general and standardised manner. The different hues, gradations, subtleties and complexities of everyday personal relationships (of couples and/or friends) tend to be ironed out of account.

For this reason the rest of the discussion will bracket out the issue of the transition from pre-modernity to modernity and concentrate attention on the interpersonal dimension of intimacy. By examining alternative analyses and sources of evidence on the nature of personal relationships in modern society, the pure relationship can be viewed in a wider perspective which makes it easier to identify some of its shortcomings.

Protective-dependent love

Reibstein has offered a view of relationships between married and/or cohabiting couples, which differs from what she regards as the some-what idealised (even 'pernicious') implications of the pure relationship (1997: 23). While based on a similar optimism about modern intimacy – such as the efficacy of committed relationships – Reibstein presents what she sees as a more 'realistic' analysis grounded in everyday relationship problems. Reibstein's pivotal claim is that what makes for a happy rela-tionship between couples over time is that they place a concern for protecting each other at the centre of their lives. Such a relationship takes the form of a protective alliance in which each partner is reliant on the other for the provision of security, loyalty and understanding. Additional factors are the willingness to give time, attention and energy to each other as well as acknowledging and appreciating each other's value. Expressing gratitude and appreciation for each other leads to a balanced 'give and take', which in turn gives rise to mutual pleasure.

This form of protective dependency derives from the model of parent–child relationships in which parents put their children's welfare centre-stage as a way of dealing with the intense dependence of the child on them in the early years. Of course, adults are not literally dependent on each other in the same ways as children are on their parents or caretak-ers. However, Reibstein is suggesting that the mutual security afforded by a protective alliance allows for a certain kind of reciprocal psycho-logical dependency that can be fruitful for intimate relationships. It enables partners to acknowledge each other's vulnerability by providing a safe and secure context in which such self and emotional exposure is possible. By appreciating the other's vulnerability each recognises their ability to hurt and wound one another. The dangerous assumption that only *you* are vulnerable, while your partner is not, is thus dismantled.

Protective dependency therefore makes for a truly supportive basis for close personal relationships. It produces the kind of psycho-emotional interdependence that allows genuine mutuality to thrive.

Reibstein is keen to establish the distinctiveness of her position, suggesting that her book flies in the face of much current thinking in so far as she claims that people *should* need to depend on each other. This is the opposite of the predominant cultural stress on the value of independence – an ideal that is also espoused by feminism and psychoanalysis. In fact, the striving for independence and the conventional equation of 'maturity' with self-reliance is one of the main reasons why couple intimacy is experiencing so many problems and difficulties. The latter, as evidenced in high divorce rates, and the rising number of affairs – especially among women – are, for Reibstein, the result of the modern tendency to regard dependence as pathological rather than normal. In this light protective-dependent love is seen as weak and regressive. Dependence is a dirty word. In order to overcome such tendencies Reibstein suggests that we need to redefine adult love by placing the need for protection at its centre, thus making the impulse to be in love in a protective way, normal (1997: 10).

Indeed, the reason why so many modern marriages and partnerships are in trouble is that they are failing to provide a protective alliance. Reibstein points to evidence that suggests that even those who stay married for a lifetime together regard their relationships as 'just alright' and that in many long-term marriages the expectation is that partners will settle for less and less. Typically, couples will arrive at a situation where they begin to ask questions like 'whatever happened to the boy/girl I once knew?' or, 'how have we ended up politely co-existing like this?' At the same time these same people are reluctant to say they are 'unhappy' and, therefore, they have no real right to complain.

Of course, there are more persistent and long-term problems facing couples, often resulting in unambiguous unhappiness and which may, in fact, signal the end of the relationship. Such a state of affairs is the result of what Reibstein refers to as a 'downward spiral' in an intimate relationship. But leaving aside those relationships that are irretrievably broken, Reibstein notes that, at various times, most close relationships undergo upward and downward spirals of a less extreme form (1997: 145–64). Downward spirals may be initiated by what she calls 'unavoidable obstacles' and 'transition points' which include divided loyalties (between partner's families), the birth of child, the middle years of childrearing and the post children phase. They may also be caused by 'abnormal crises' such as illness, disability, death or unexpected losses (of job or home). To these I would add important phenomena such as partners growing apart in their interests or goals, or the emotional drift caused by habituation and familiarity (Duncombe and Marsden 1995).

According to Reibstein, to save or resuscitate relationships in trouble, the therapeutic task is to transform downward spirals into upward ones, and this can only be achieved by endeavouring to make a protective alliance the heart of the relationship if it wasn't in the first place, or to restore it if it was in disrepair. The nature of such therapeutic aims is not presently of central interest (although I have more to say about some of the hidden dangers of protective-dependent love in Chapter 11). However, of great importance is Reibstein's acknowledgement that downward and upward spirals are routine features of intimate relationships. This is crucial in distinguishing her position on modern intimacy from that associated with the pure relationship.

Indeed, according to Reibstein, the ideology of independence enshrined in the notion of the pure relationship is an important reason why it is a struggle to stay in love. She suggests that the pure relationship rests on the 'insidious idea that the romance which set off the courtship remains the spark plug of the relationship' (1997: 23). Whether or not such a relationship works is measured in terms of 'how good does it make me feel?' and this becomes the criterion for its continued existence. But, says Reibstein, a host of social problems are created by the instability caused by modern relationships failing to measure up to such stringent standards. By contrast, modern relationships are 'under siege' much of the time and 'even happy couples experience periods of being disgruntled with the quality of their relationships'. In this sense relationships do not automatically 'work' nor is mutual satisfaction automatically achieved. The reality of modern relationships involves acknowledging the problems arising from 'day to day rubbing along together'. These can only be overcome through continuous delicate negotiations pivoting 'around the idea that each partner needs and wants protection from the other' (1997: 24).

Clearly, Reibstein's notion of protective-dependent love is directed against some of the idealised assumptions built into the notion of the pure relationship. By suggesting that the everyday reality of modern intimacy is a fairly messy and pragmatic affair, Reibstein's approach opens up the possibility that close relationships are many-sided. That modern intimacy is ambiguous, complex and problematic makes for a stark contrast with the idealised 'purity' of the pure relationship. A crucial point is that Reibstein contends that a routine feature of even 'happy' relationships is their propensity to experience upward and downward spirals. In my opinion this suggests that close relationships may take on transitional forms – and I shall take up this idea later in the discussion.

The idea that intimacy both requires and is, therefore, the result of continuous negotiations centring on the needs and problems of partners 'rubbing along together' also open up the possibility that trust, commitment and 'satisfaction' may vary. It is also consistent with the idea that they vary according to the interpersonal 'state of play' in a relationship at any one point in time. Indeed, 'time' as it is reflected in the gradual unfolding (or thwarting) of close relationships suggests that modern intimacy is best understood as a graded, many-sided and ever-developing interpersonal process. There is nothing unified and fixed about intimacy.

Types of love and intimacy

Marshall's (2006) study of couples presents a similar kind of analysis to that of Reibstein by concentrating on the practical, everyday realities and problems of sustaining optimal intimacy over time. However, Marshall's realism is even more pronounced and, if anything, veers more towards the pessimistic side than Reibstein. While Marshall shares a concern about trying to rescue troubled relationships (he too is a marital therapist), he gives greater weight to the difficulties that lie in the way of intimate relationships. Marshall's approach is driven by the question – 'what happens when the passion goes?'

In this sense Marshall is concerned with how couples deal with their relationship after the initial passionate absorption in each other has – inevitably – waned, and how they face having to adjust to the rather hum-drum problems of daily life. All too often, observes Marshall, partnerships become defined by companionship rather than passion (even though sex may still play a part). These people often still cared about each other but they (or just one of them) had fallen out of love and though not wishing to hurt anyone, wanted to end the relationship. These are the kinds of relationships that Marshall feels are summarised in terms of the phrase 'I love you, but I'm not in love with you'.

Marshall suggests we can understand what happens here by making some distinctions between different kinds of 'love'. First, love may be defined in terms of the early days of 'honey moon' passion (referred to as 'limerence') which lasts between a year and eighteen months. This is characterised by a tendency for the couple to merge into a 'oneness', in which sexual activity is intense and where 'all differences are overlooked or ignored as two people blend into one' (Marshall 2006: 31). After this, what Marshall calls 'loving attachment' usually takes over. The magic and brilliance of limerence is not enough to sustain a relationship, something more is needed. An unfortunate myth about romantic love is contained in the idea that once we have found our partner we can relax and that love will automatically help us through any problems. However, in the state of limerence, lovers are bound to each other no matter how badly they behave, and tend to see each other's weaknesses as strengths. This contrasts with 'loving attachment', which needs to be worked at, otherwise it will die. This is made all the more acute because as couples become long term they become aware of the need to accommodate their partner's differences and weaknesses in order to sustain intimacy. Also, loving attachment demands that the couple begin to grapple with the complexities of life and its practical demands (such as work, having children and so on) and this requires rather more than their love 'to keep them warm'.

If the couple don't develop the necessary skills to sustain intimacy as relationships develop from limerence to loving attachment, then the quality of their loving attachment itself may suffer. When this is the case 'love' may be transformed into a third type – 'affectionate regard' which is generally what we feel for parents, children, siblings and best friends. This kind of love makes us want to care for someone, but we do not feel that our destiny is entwined with theirs in the same way as with loving attachment. Marshall says that in the 'I love you but I'm not in love with you' syndrome, the 'I love you' invariably means 'I have affectionate regard for you'.

As noted, those who feel that their relationship has dwindled into this state often want to end it because it lacks passionate fulfilment and emotional satisfaction. On the other hand, for a host of reasons, many people endure such an unsatisfactory state of affairs whilst building up resentment and anger towards their partner. In such relationships there is a loss of communication, an inability to reach out to the other either physically or emotionally, and a tendency to detach and drift apart. Very often there is 'polite sex' rather than 'intimate love making' and the couple may even 'consider their marriage to be good even if the lovemaking is routine and unfulfilled' (2006: 109).

Marshall notes that issues around self-identity and difference often characterise relationships like this. One aspect of this is that some couples avoid open confrontation and pretend that their differences do not exist. But by not acknowledging differences, and confronting the ones that cause trouble, it is easy to let the relationship drift. Another related problem is that that either one or both will complain of having become a rather amorphous couple and losing their identity as a consequence. They fail to strike the balance between finding enough similarities with their partner to sustain a long-term connection while, at the same time, having enough differences from them in order to stop the relationship stagnating. Some 'friction' based on difference between partners provides the spark of passion (Perel 2007). Yet another cause (or indeed consequence) for relationship stagnation of this kind involves the kind of emotional infidelity that arises from 'inappropriate friendships'.

Successful, happy couples are those who have learnt to allow each other a measure of independence, to compromise over their differences and take risks (instead of being defensive and putting up barriers). They also tend to set aside time for one another, to have a laugh together, and through action rather than words, demonstrate their affection for each other (Marshall 2006: 183–93). Without these skills intimate relationships are likely to become soured and clogged with resentments and hurts. As with Reibstein's analysis, but with more emphasis on its pitfalls and downsides, Marshall's analysis opens up the possibility that intimate relationships are more complex and variable than envisaged in the pure relationship.

Intimate terrorism

On the basis of his own research evidence, Miller (1995) takes this kind of approach yet another step further down the road of pessimism about modern couple intimacy. He suggests that today relationships are best characterised by the term 'intimate terrorism' which conveys the dissolution of the myth of romantic love which has been influential for so long. Drawing on psychology, sociology and literature as well as his therapeutic practice, Miller argues that modern intimacy has become contaminated by power and struggles for power in relationships. In this sense Miller paints a picture that is a far cry from the ideal of the pure relationship with its preoccupation with egalitarianism and intimacy as a vehicle for emotional satisfaction. Now I don't agree that modern intimacy should be characterised *entirely* by the notion of emotional terrorism as Miller seems to suggest, but his account provides an important corrective to the overly optimistic and idealised notion of the pure relationship. Also, Miller's emphasis on the importance of the relation between power and love is one that clearly resonates with the wider framework of my argument.

Although a concern with power and control is undoubtedly crucial and leads Miller to deal with some interesting aspects of the use and misuse of power in intimacy, I substantially disagree with the way in which he defines power and control and their relation to intimacy. Succinctly put, Miller's account does not allow for the existence of benign forms of power and control that are absolutely pivotal to my own account. He follows so many writers on power by mistakenly construing it in entirely negative terms and, thus, *in opposition* to love (and intimacy). In this sense for Miller, love or intimacy is different from power since power is manipulative and exploitative whilst love, on the other hand, 'cannot be controlled; it is freely given, or it becomes little more than a coerced charade' (1995: 31).

But this is a skewed account of power. In a general sense, power is an abstract *capacity*; it is not a particular kind of behaviour or an outcome of that behaviour. That is, power is about the *ability* to do things, transform circumstances or bring about change. Thus, power and control may be in the service of either benign or malign intentions, and their behavioural consequences. In this sense benign forms of power and control are essential to the capacity for love and for the caring responses that go with it. Only through interpersonal influence and control (as reflected in the capacity for love and empathy and so on) can a person elicit loving responses from another, and thus create and sustain a close personal relationship. It is only manipulative forms of power and control – those that ride roughshod over the wishes, desires and intentions of others – that are inimical to intimacy. Thus, a certain kind of power and control is *generative* of love and intimacy, while other kinds diminish or undermine them.

It is important to bear this distinction in mind when making global statements about the relation of power and intimacy of the kind Miller makes. In this light we have to severely qualify Miller's claims that 'the confusion of love and power can be damaging to both relationships and individuals' and that 'being able to distinguish between the relative proportions of love and power in any relationship seems to me essential to the health of the relationship' (1995: 24). Clearly, love cannot be coerced or controlled in a manipulative or exploitative sense, but it is impossible for intimacy to be created or sustained without the interpersonal influence of benign power and control. Thus it is emphatically not a matter of confusing power with love, but of confusing love with a certain kind of power. Bearing in mind this problematic but crucial matter, let us examine the core of Miller's arguments.

Modern relationships and intimate terrorism

A couple is engaged in intimate terrorism when their more usual day-to-day concerns – with finances, moods, love-making and so on – have become contaminated and overtaken by a power struggle for control of the relationship. Although the struggle may seem to be a response to disappointments, misunderstandings and grievances, Miller argues that the main culprit is the expansion of anxiety that 'plagues all erotic love'. In this context, 'intimate partners get trapped in a vicious cycle of complementary anxieties – fears each has of either being abandoned or engulfed by the other' (1995:28). Abandonment anxiety is based on the fear of occupying a void left behind by the departure of another, while engulfment anxiety is the fear of being swallowed up or dominated by the other's constant needs.

In intimate terrorism the partners are preoccupied with attacking one another's autonomy and security and although neither of them is ready to give up the other 'each has the aim of seizing control of the relationship' (1995: 30) in order to make it seem more safe and predictable. In this sense anxiety results in an attempt to control what cannot be controlled, because, as Miller rightly points out, love cannot be controlled. Abandonment and engulfment anxieties create a profound sense of powerlessness. Efforts to seize control of the relationship represent an attempt to overcome feelings of powerlessness. Miller says that these power struggles rarely show up at first 'because infatuation and courtship are so mutually satisfying, but they often surface once the relationship becomes a matter of daily living' (1995: 31).

An interesting point raised here is the idea that such relationships are not necessarily abandoned. This contrasts sharply with the idea (implicit in the pure relationship) that modern intimacy stands and falls in terms of whether it provides mutual (positive) psycho-emotional satisfaction. Failure in this respect usually means the end of the relationship and a search for a new partner. Miller is suggesting that many couples become locked together in a state of intimate terrorism – as a normal or routine form of co-existence. If anything, such a state of affairs could only sustain a very negative sense of 'mutual satisfaction'. But this, indeed, is what Miller understands as the function of intimate terrorism. It is about the need for coexistence however unpeaceful this may be. Intimate terrorism keeps the relationship together, 'even if this can be accomplished only through suffering and coercion rather than pleasure and choice' (1995: 36).

In this sense, 'the manipulation of anxiety replaces love as the chief means of social cohesion. It works because love and anxiety are so closely allied, and when love fails to bind us to another person, anxiety can fulfil the same function.' As Miller puts it, 'you could say that intimate terrorism is the dark underside of love, a form of negative love. It consists of two people clinging to one another in an atmosphere of mutual intimidation' (1995: 37). Partners in such a situation realise they are creating their own misery but are no longer sure about whether they are choosing to stick together. Instead, they both feel 'stuck' – in a prison of their own making. They feel that there are no options open to them – they can't part, but neither can they live together differently – even though each may spend a good deal of time fantasising about such possibilities.

The desire for commitment, security and trust in the context of a meaningful relationship remains strong, but when love disappears the partners prefer to settle for intimate terrorism, rather than experience the aloneness of separation. The pleasure of loving exchanges is replaced by strategies of power and control, which provide an equivalent sense of 'intense relatedness'. Here, clearly, notions of commitment, satisfaction, trust and so on become transformed into hybrid forms to replace the earlier ones, while continuing to serve the same function of keeping the relationship together – albeit in a rather destructive context.

It is interesting to compare Miller's account of modern intimacy – as typified by intimate terrorism – in relation to my own. Further on I describe six types of intimate relationship reflecting the plurality and complexity of modern intimacy. Elements of all six types can be discerned in the different empirically based studies reviewed here. In this respect Miller's discussion of intimate terrorism is too generalised. Characterising modern intimacy entirely as intimate terrorism is an over-simplification that fails to acknowledge or register the nuances, subtleties and complexities involved in close relationships today. In that sense it is the obverse of the pure relationship account – it simply replaces one over-general account with another, equally general one. However, the undoubted usefulness and importance of the idea of intimate terrorism lies in its portrayal of the opposite end of the spectrum of intimacy to that of the pure relationship. This is evident both in its pessimism and in its depiction of an alternative range of possibilities.

With regard to the broad spectrum (the six types) of intimate relationship that I identify, intimate terrorism seems pertinent to several of them. For my purposes it is more appropriate to think in terms of *degrees* of intimate terrorism ranging from milder to more volatile forms.

With reference to the latter, Miller often seems to be talking about what I call 'manipulative' or 'oppressive' types of intimacy – those in which exploitative power and control is most evident. By way of contrast, some of his examples of intimate terrorism come from the 'milder' end of the spectrum and are thus more pertinent to what I call 'episodic', 'semi-detached' or 'pretence intimacy' in which there still remains some (if only residual) evidence of benign power and control. Of course, this underlines the importance of the distinction between different types of power (which Miller overlooks), for an overall understanding of the full range of types of intimate relationship.

An ever-present background to Miller's account of intimate terrorism is a focus on the 'disappointments inherent in marriage itself' or in how 'romantic love has failed us' (1995: 79). Partly, disappointment is the result of the unrealistic burden of expectations placed on love and marriage. More pragmatically, some degree of disappointment inevitably sets in once the initial passion has run its course, and this poses the question of how couples deal with it. Often, relationships beset by bitter irreconcilable quarrels don't simply end with the partners heading for the divorce courts. Instead, in many cases, 'the war gradually attenuates into a standoff, and the relationship, drained of vitality and meaning, continues to exist in sullen climate of alienation and chronic discontent' (1995: 80).

Another theme is the way in which troubled couples attempt to create a safety zone in which they can protect themselves from too much closeness and too much aloneness by 'carefully editing their intimacy, perhaps allowing close companionable affection with infrequent or no sex', or having 'lots of sex with little or no demonstrable affection out of bed' (1995: 123). This, of course, is an attempt to create a semblance of security in an environment of disappointment, sometimes even of despair. But it is, ultimately, an empty security based on the maintenance of a protective distance between them. They go through fluctuating periods of relative quiet, 'quarrels, affairs, confessions and reconciliations, bouts of weeping and hurling ashtrays' (1995: 133). Affairs are important both in driving a wedge between the partners and in creating 'a buffer of safety from intimacy' (1995: 136).

The experience of failure and disappointment and the ways in which couples try to deal with them by creating a buffer zone, which both keeps them together and keeps them apart at the same time, echo some of the themes indicated by Marshall. More generally, they speak to the way in which intimacy may unravel over time. But as I have already intimated, these themes are relevant not only to the extremes of intimate terrorism. In what I refer to as 'manipulative' and 'oppressive' types of intimacy, exploitative power and control are at the fore. Themes of alienation, distancing, editing intimacy and so on are also very much part of 'episodic', 'semi-detached' and 'pretence' intimacy. In these types, couples attempts to deal with each other retain some vestige of benignity. Again, 'intimate terrorism' is too blanket a term to deal with the transitional and intermediary stages in the unravelling or transformation of intimacy – a process which traces the move from a relatively benign, to a more insidious and exploitative state of interpersonal affairs.

Disclosure, inequality and disappointment

The foregoing discussion of the works of Reibstein, Marshall and Miller suggests that certain aspects of modern intimacy do not fit comfortably with those implied in the pure relationship. In this section I examine the work that is even more directly critical of it. On the basis of an extensive review of studies of intimacy from the whole spectrum (that is, including parent–children, kin and same sex relationships), Jamieson (1998, 1999) suggests that modern relationships are not moving towards the pure relationship based on the gender equality of the partners, as Giddens assumes. Instead, there remain persistent inequalities of gender that continue to influence intimate relationships. However, despite this, she argues that modern intimate relationships are often more concerned with 'a range of creative identity and relationship *saving* strategies' (my emphasis) and that 'perhaps much more creative energy goes into *sustaining a sense of intimacy* despite inequality' (Jamieson 1998, my emphasis).

However, it is possible to understand these phenomena in more than one way. Jamieson sees them as most relevant where gender inequalities work to unsettle the quality of intimacy in particular relationships. Thus, 'identity and relationship saving strategies' and 'sustaining a sense of intimacy' play important roles in propping up strained, persistently troubled relationships, which might otherwise split asunder. In this sense, 'sustaining a sense of intimacy' literally means creating a façade or pretence of closeness in situations where it is clearly lacking.

But there are other more positive ways in which these phenomena may be understood, especially in relation to couples experiencing upward and downward spirals as Reibstein refers to them. Even optimal intimacy (what I call dynamic intimacy) is not without its ups and downs, its fair share of arguments and spats. Periodic upheavals and conflicts are a routine feature of even the best intimacy. Here the idea of 'sustaining a sense of intimacy' refers to the active and creative strategies that keep a relationship vibrant by feeding the flow of benign power and influence that energises successful intimacy. It refers to the emotion work required from partners that is essential to maintaining the vibrancy of intimate relationships.

Jamieson also suggests that the 'disclosing intimacy' implicit in the pure relationship is not the dominant type of intimacy in most couple relationships. She emphasises a gender dimension here, citing Duncombe and Marsden's (1995) finding that men lack emotional openness and that they were unwilling to participate in disclosing intimacy. She also adds that there is much evidence of 'men's under-participation in more practical loving and caring'. She concludes that

> for most couples, intimacy was intertwined with and expressed through practical arrangements of who did the household chores, who spent what money and the like. Men and women did not bracket off these aspects of their relationship in how they viewed each other but saw them as part of how they loved or did not love each other.
>
> (1998: 157)

Apart from practical care and support, Jamieson also notes that intimacy can be conveyed through means other than self-disclosure, for example through 'silent intimacy' where nothing much is said although the partners 'express' love and care through, for example, physical presence or acts of loyalty. The question of the variable nature of disclosure in intimacy is important in distinguishing between the different types I describe later in the chapter. I shall come back to this after reviewing some of Craib's (1992, 1994, 1998) criticisms of the pure relationship.

Craib questions the central role that 'emotional satisfaction' plays in the pure relationship. He notes that if there is, indeed, any such thing as emotional satisfaction, it is of a transient nature. When its effects have peaked, so to speak, it is always followed by its opposite, the feeling of dissatisfaction. In this sense satisfaction and dissatisfaction go hand in hand – 'simple satisfaction is never possible' (1994: 123). The idea of complete satisfaction, especially in intimacy, always remains a fantasy never a reality, and to expect or demand it from our relationships is to seek the impossible. Crucially, Craib suggests that imagining that complete satisfaction is the goal of our relationships prevents us learning from them – psychologically and emotionally – when they fail, or when love disappears. Instead of enriching our knowledge of intimacy, people and the world around us, the decline of love is experienced as personal failure and deficiency.

Second, Craib points out that emotional satisfaction is not always pleasant. There are times when talking to each other (self-disclosure) actually makes things worse rather than better. Sometimes emotional satisfaction involves 'rows attacks, hurting and being hurt; this is part and parcel of intimacy' (1994: 124). Craib's point is not that emotional satisfaction isn't part of intimate relationships, but that it is fragile, unstable and contradictory and can involve negative and destructive dimensions. Indeed, the very act of falling in love is usually followed by a degree of disillusion when our partner fails to live up to the role we have assigned to them. In this respect we should not approach relationships without the expectation of being unhappy for some of the time. Craib isn't saying that mutually destructive unhappiness should be borne or endured or be better ended. Rather he's pointing out that the simple appearance of unhappiness should not be the reason for raising the possibility of ending the relationship. An essential part of this is that in any relationship there will be 'complex inequalities of effort' and in which 'partners must be willing to exploit the other and be exploited for periods'. In a long-term relationship, 'hate can play as big a part as love, and the relationship can contain passionate expressions of both' (1994: 128).

Finally, Craib claims that 'the level of self-revelation in a normal relationship has to be limited to make it work' (1994: 130). It is not necessarily good for partners to tell each other every time they found other people attractive, or if they always tell each other what they cannot stand about each other. Sometimes it is important 'not to talk', especially where this helps to avoid hurtful comments, unreasonable demands or unwarranted attacks on the other. This continues the theme raised in Jamieson's work that self-disclosure in intimacy is much more variable than that envisaged in the pure relationship. The extent and nature of disclosure varies according to different types of intimacy.

Types of intimacy

In the following sections I outline six types of intimate relationship, which build upon the idea that intimacy is much more variable and complex than is presupposed in the notion of the pure relationship. The preceding discussion of 'alternative' accounts of the nature of modern intimacy, and the evidence on which they are based, indicates the existence of such variability. In my opinion the findings reported in these accounts are entirely consistent with, and provide the substantive basis for, the typology of intimate relationships developed here. (Although none of the accounts is organised in terms of different types of intimacy.) The types are defined by the presence of several variable characteristics of intimate relationships. These include the nature and extent of disclosure, commitment, trust and sincerity; the emotional atmosphere; the extent of emotional and sexual infidelity; the focus or orientation of the partners; the nature of communication between them; how 'satisfaction' is defined within the relationship. The full range of types commonly found in couples (and to a lesser extent in friendship) is as follows:

Dynamic
Episodic
Semi-detached
Pretence
Manipulative
Oppressive

Dynamic, episodic and semi-detached types cluster together, indicating how they are, or may be, linked. Dynamic intimacy represents the optimal form of intimacy – in which partners experience a high degree of mutual satisfaction. The episodic and semi-detached types trace a progressive decrease in the quality of intimacy as the partners become more and more dissatisfied with the arrangement. Clearly, some elements of this 'trajectory' are documented in the findings of Reibstein, Marshall, Craib and Miller although none of them distinguish between types of intimacy. As already briefly mentioned in relation to Reibstein's work, regardless of how successful they are, all relationships routinely experience upward and downward changes in the quality of intimacy and the degree of harmony of the partners.

By identifying episodic and semi-detached intimacy as 'depreciated' forms of dynamic intimacy, we can begin to understand changes in intimate behaviour in terms of transitions between these types. There are two possible sorts of transition. The first traces an inexorable decline in a relationship (which may be gradual or rapid), and involves a move from dynamic through to episodic and then to semi-detached intimacy. If the couple don't split up, a relationship like this may deteriorate even further, ending up as mutual pretence, manipulation or oppressive intimacy (or a combination of them). On the other hand, transitions may be associated with what Reibstein refers to as upward and downward spirals in relationships. For example, this might involve a movement from dynamic, to episodic, to semi-detached and back up to dynamic (or episodic) as partners overcome (fully or partly) their problems. Clearly, some relationships do not 'fit' just one type of intimacy – they may contain overlapping aspects of several types of intimacy. Thus, for example, elements of the manipulative or pretence types might co-exist with aspects of episodic, semi-detached, even, dynamic intimacy.

The following descriptions of different types of intimacy have been generated by a process of abstraction from the empirical findings of studies such as those of Reibstein, Marshall, Miller, Craib (and others) based on interviews, conversations with hundreds of couples, as well as drawing on the authors' therapeutic and counselling experience. It is important to remember that this process means that my typological descriptions sometimes depart from, and in a sense 'go beyond', the original explanatory remit, or framework of the authors.

Dynamic intimacy

Relationships are never a harmonious balance of love, care and support. However, overall dynamic intimacy has a good emotional atmosphere, with negativity and unresolved conflicts playing only a minor role. Neither partner dominates. Instead, they either share or regularly swap control with each having an opportunity to be 'in the driving seat'. As Craib (1994: 128) says, this often involves 'complex inequalities of effort' in which 'partners must be willing to exploit the other and be exploited for periods'. Beyond this, partners encourage one another's freedom and independence to pursue separate interests, friendships and contact with kin or work colleagues. They also allow one another to grow independently, as individuals (Fromm 1971). In this sense, self-development works to strengthen bonds because it encourages greater self-disclosure.

Discussion is open and free – although this doesn't prevent arguments, conflict and misunderstanding as part of the routine 'rough and tumble' of a close relationship. Openness, mutual freedom and self-development lead to feelings of sincerity and trust. As Reibstein (1997) has noted, such feelings are associated with the relationship as a 'protective alliance', which makes partners feel 'grateful for, and pleasure in, one another'. Although closeness, care and support are at the forefront of partner's concerns, some deception (as in 'white lies'), mistrust and insincerity are inevitable. These are best understood as instances of 'soft manipulation', which plays an important part in mutual benign control and is nowhere near as destructive as 'pure' manipulation.

Soft manipulation involves guiding someone in the direction you want them to go because it is in their, and your, best interests. Among other things, it involves gently persuading them to fall in with an enterprise not of their own making, but which they come to see as desirable. An example of this would be getting a partner to change an aspect of their behaviour – say an annoying habit or their 'obstinate' views. This may involve major or minor matters – ranging from bad dress sense, whether or not to have children, to quit smoking or drinking, to relax 'house-rules' as children get older, or even to change a sexual preference. The change is accomplished without threats or guilt trips and without trampling on the other's interests or desires. He or she is brought 'on-side' by persuasion, cajoling, teasing or bargaining.

Crucially in dynamic intimacy, open discussion permits a free exchange of ideas and feelings about intensely personal matters. Because of mutual trust, partners are willing to open-up without fear of recrimination and this 'freedom' continually revitalises the bond. Spontaneous open discussion like this is the polar opposite of one or both partners 'insisting' that the other 'tells them everything' and where 'conversation' bears a striking resemblance to interrogation.

Episodic intimacy

'Dynamic intimacy' is mostly close and harmonious – occasionally interrupted by arguments and disagreements. In contrast, 'episodic intimacy' is more disrupted and less intense. Evidence of this type of intimacy is amply illustrated in the studies of Reibstein, Miller and Marshall. It might seem like 'second rate' intimacy but this depends on partner's feelings. If both are happy with this state of affairs, then there is no problem. It might also be acceptable if both partners (couples or friends) are not exactly happy, but are prepared to tolerate the situation – perhaps because they don't expect anything more, or because it suits their current needs. In either case, 'episodic intimacy' is intimacy that has deteriorated over time.

This type usually emerges later on in a relationship if partners have partly withdrawn their energies but retain some commitment to the relationship. This is often recognisable in couples for whom, and for whatever reason, the full bloom of love has not survived beyond the early period of intense and focused passion. Instead, the relationship has evolved, largely unconsciously, into a set of compromises and routines.

The partners are living virtually separately, but still want to keep the relationship going as a basic anchor for their lives.

From time to time, partners are caring, supportive and loving. They are generally courteous and occasionally flatter one another, offering gifts, sex, companionship and so on. Of course, these may also be used 'manipulatively' as ploys to keep the relationship 'ticking over', and to preserve its outward appearance. In this sense intimacy is used selectively to 'manage' problems that may threaten the relationship. This happens, for instance, when couples offer sex as a substitute for conversation or emotional disclosure. If sex is off the agenda, gifts may serve to offset the lack of emotional connection. Selective intimacy like this may be relatively 'silent' so as to avoid more revealing disclosures that may occur inadvertently through talk.

Generally in episodic intimacy, disclosure is less authentic. Emotional commitment has declined, and partners are less open with each other. This creates a psychological and emotional space that allows them to 'engage at a distance' without appearing too insincere, which is important because they still need to trust one another to some extent. Discussion is much less free but not because one partner wants to dominate proceedings or block information. Rather, it is because they both selectively withhold their feelings. Such a state of affairs can lead to estrangement between couples and gives rise to comments like that from one of Reibstein's female interviewees when she says of her husband:

> he acts as if I don't exist. When I walk into a room and all I want to do is have a chat, tell him about how my day has gone, what the children are up to, all that kind of stuff, he sits and reads the paper as if I'm not even there! He doesn't love me. If he loved me he would want to listen to me, talk to me about himself. He would want to spend time with me.
>
> (Reibstein 1997: 13)

Such a lack of rapport is seriously damaging, of course, but doesn't completely destroy the sincerity and trust that cradle relationships like this. In fact, if partners want to keep the benefits of a protective alliance – at least *some* trust and sincerity are necessary. Thus, instead of disappearing completely, trust and sincerity become hollowed out. The result is that the partners themselves become less and less the main focus of the relationship. Although some trust remains they no longer see one another as its main focus. Trust is increasingly invested in others outside the pair bond. The once focal partner is now only one of a number of others with whom 'trust commitments' are made.

In this respect emotional affairs or emotional infidelity – the sharing of intimate experiences with, say, work friends, rather than partners – which has been made easier through texts, e-mails and the Internet – take on an increasing importance. (It may, in effect, be the half-way stage to full-on sexual infidelity.) Along with such changes, the sincerity that once cocooned the relationship undergoes a shift of emphasis. Partners deal with one another less 'authentically'. Their intimacy is more 'performed' and manipulative because they no longer see one another as the only 'source' of emotional satisfaction.

Marshall's (2006) findings indicate the existence of many couples like this who remain together in spite of a lack of passion in their relationships and their dissatisfaction with the companionate nature of their everyday life. This suggests a distinction between 'true' companionate relationships in which both partners are happy to settle for this state of affairs (noted by Giddens 1992: 155), and 'pseudo' companionate bonds that have become so by default because the partners have drifted apart emotionally. For Marshall these relationships exemplify the theme of partners 'loving' each other, but not being 'in love'.

Although this kind of intimacy mainly occurs in the 'second phase' of a relationship, on occasion, partners may choose it from the start. Sometimes friends or family members, even couples, want a less intense relationship because they feel happier in less 'demanding' and focused relationships. Episodic intimacy allows more space and independence and releases them from the 'tyranny of responsibilities' that comes with the more full-on styles. Of course, a relationship that starts out like this will only continue to work while both partners feel the same about it. If one person decides that she or he wants better intimacy they may, in fact, decide to end the relationship. But there are definite benefits with the episodic style that shouldn't be underestimated. Restrained intimacy of this kind is necessary if partners are uncomfortable with full-on closeness, but – for whatever reason – want to keep the relationship going.

Semi-detached intimacy

This type is yet another step away from dynamic intimacy, and again, usually occurs in the later phases of a relationship. Intimacy may become semi-detached if one or both partners privately desire greater closeness, but also realise it isn't currently possible. Full intimacy may be kept at arm's length for any number of reasons – perhaps because of bottled-up anger, or frustration at having always to make the first move. Whatever the reason, disappointment at the way things have turned out will give rise to (mainly) unspoken resentments. If only one of the partners feels this way, then he or she will become emotionally semi-detached. Their partner may not even notice or turn a blind eye, although both settle for a second-rate intimacy.

Sometimes both partners withdraw emotionally because of the hurt caused by unresolved issues and conflicts. Semi-detached intimacy allows a 'convenient' co-existence in which the partners simply carry on together either out of sheer inertia or lack of options. If the desire for greater closeness becomes more urgent, it may cause conflict, and tension. Partners might then seek satisfaction through emotional or sexual affairs while keeping the relationship going in name only. The kind of situation to which this may give rise is illustrated in a letter written by a married woman and published anonymously in the *Times* newspaper. She tells of the terrible consequences of an affair with a man she felt was the love of her life and says that it 'exposed the sham that is my marriage'. However, she explains that the affair did not last and she and her lover parted painfully because they 'lacked the courage to upset so many other lives'. After the affair her marriage was never the same again. Her emotional energy is constantly diverted away from her marriage and sex had become an act of 'mechanics' rather than 'affirmation'. She says 'we now keep each other at a respectful distance. . . . we veer away from anything that would mean engaging at a deeper level and live in a vacuum of emotional sterility' (*Times* 2007).

In general, with semi-detached intimacy disclosure is rare, and sometimes entirely absent. The partners largely 'act-out' or 'perform' intimacy, although not always in a wholly deliberate or false way. Often, they will 'go through the motions', half-believing that their 'original' feelings may reappear and be revitalised. Mostly, however, their disappointments are confirmed. Occasionally, fleeting moments of intimacy may occur by chance when partners stumble across common ground, or share some satisfying experience. This creates a brief spark of closeness, a reminder of what has been, what might have been, and what could be, if only the barriers could be removed. Often, though, such occasions are met with embarrassment and unease. The chance of a revival of feelings is lost and the partners return to their habits of non-disclosure.

With semi-detached intimacy the emotional drift between partners is almost permanent and very obvious to all. The dissatisfaction bred by this leads to a search for fulfilment beyond the confines of the relationship. Of course, emotional and sexual infidelity only widens the gulf between the partners because alliances outside the relationship shatter any remaining pretence of a protective alliance. Since partners' attention is focused outside the bond, semi-detached intimacy frequently involves manipulation, deception, insincerity and mistrust.

Pretence intimacy

In relationships like this intimacy has deteriorated into sheer pretence. The research on which Miller bases his study of 'intimate terrorism' is replete with examples of couples that fit this type of 'intimacy'. In a sense these couples are preoccupied with 'putting on a show' – and this may be harmless enough if neither partner really cares. However, if there is underlying resentment, say, about being trapped in a loveless marriage (or a family betrayal), pretence intimacy may mask real anger, jealousy and bitterness. As such, this type prevents real but unexpressed feelings breaking through.

   More often than not, for couples, pretence intimacy is the natural end point for a relationship in trouble and on the decline – perhaps already having passed through episodic and semi-detached intimacy on the way. The partners are fully detached from each other psychologically, but for various reasons (the sake of the children, fear of loneliness, loss of financial or social status) they remain together in an emotional wasteland. Genuine intimacy is not on the agenda so that mutual pretence allows personal engagement 'without tears'. But the surface display is underpinned by anger, tensions and suppressed conflict. Often there is a silent war of attrition with each partner trying to wear the other down, or get one up. Putting one another down in company is typical, although one partner may be more vicious and determined to outdo the other. At this point pretence may slide into manipulation. In many respects this type is reflected in examples of couples, from Miller's (1995) research, engaged in the 'two person civil war' that he calls 'intimate terrorism'.

Manipulated intimacy

Here, mutual benign control gives way to 'serious' manipulation where one person (for whatever reason) wants to control the other, and again, Miller's research offers plenty of examples of this type. Predominantly, communication flows in one particular direction – from the controller to the controlled. The controller's wishes and interests come first and the whole package is sealed with insincerity and double-dealing, but stops short of physical coercion. (Although, of course, psychological manipulation might function as a way station for a physically abusive relationship; see Horley 2000.) Apparent closeness is massaged and 'managed' by the controller who, over time, convinces the partner that he or she knows best. One way of achieving this is by the subtle use of benign control. Under the disguise of 'care' and 'support', the controller's needs and desires are serviced at the expense of his or her partner. For this to work properly the controlling partner must know the other's inner thoughts and feelings very thoroughly in order to use them as tools of manipulation.

Thus the victim becomes convinced that the manipulator knows him or her better than they know themselves, and what is best for them both. But the controller simply leads the target by the nose saying things like 'you know how sensitive you are, you better leave this to me', or, 'I'm doing this for your benefit you know', 'It's you I'm concerned about', 'I didn't want to burden you with the responsibility of making that decision', 'You're happiest when I take care of you'. Although these are manipulative and deceitful, they aren't seriously malicious.

However, more bullying tactics also produce results. Thus, sulking, criticism, insults and put-downs based on intimate knowledge of a partner's weaknesses and insecurities may ensure his or her compliance – although it may be reluctantly given. Research on emotional blackmail (Forward and Frazier 1998) suggests that it is more subtle than bullying, but still depends on direct or indirect threats. It gains its force by linking personal insecurities and secrets with the threatened withdrawal of love, or abandonment. The blackmailer says things like 'After all I've done for you, you treat me like this', 'Why do you always hurt me', 'Don't bother to visit, I don't really deserve it', 'If you do this for me it will prove you love me and in return I'll love you forever'. Emotional blackmailers are fearful and insecure, and use emotional manipulation to make themselves feel powerful.

While the victim is encouraged to disclose her or his vulnerabilities, the manipulator is careful to conceal personally sensitive information, to ensure that his or her own power position isn't threatened. Clearly, there is no 'free' discussion of feelings or opinions, and the cards are continually stacked against the weaker partner. Manipulated intimacy of this kind is found in many relationships (couples, families and friends) often alongside other styles. For example, it is common for milder forms of emotional blackmail and emotional bullying to occur with dynamic, episodic and semi-detached intimacy.

Oppressive intimacy

Sometimes referred to as 'co-dependence', some of the characteristics of oppressive intimacy are fairly well documented (Peele and Brodsky 1974, Person 1990, Giddens 1992). Partners in oppressive intimacy are fairly equally matched and manipulate each other. But both are insecure and over-reliant on the other to boost their confidence and self-esteem. They only feel secure when they are together and are therefore anxious about allowing one another to have 'outside' relationships with friends, or even family. Thus the individuality and independence of both partners is sacrificed in favour of their bond. And, although it may provide a defence against loneliness and anxiety, the relationship is excessively close, suffocating and oppressive.

Partners' reliance on one another is addictive (Peele and Brodsky 1974). They rarely spend time outside one another's company, so avoiding the threat that others may pose. Of course, this unduly limits their freedom and personal development and is quite the opposite of 'healthy love' in Fromm's (1971) terms. To make sure there are no betrayals, partners closely monitor each other's behaviour at all times with the consequence that disclosure is forced, rather than freely given. Partners are 'required' to report on the minutiae of their daily lives and thus there is a 'confessional' feel to disclosure instead of a genuine sharing of feelings. The suffocating and oppressive atmosphere creates fragile and potentially volatile relationships. If one partner seeks to escape from the claustrophobia, it will upset the control balance and may lead to a struggle for power. The now weaker partner may fight to gain control and boost his or her self-esteem.

Another variant arises when a needy partner becomes excessively dependent. The stronger partner may have no wish to dominate the relationship but he or she might find this over-dependence tiresome and oppressive. If anything, the weaker partner may turn out to be the manipulative one, smothering the other with a clingy intense love, constantly off-loading emotionally, but giving little or nothing in return. Alternatively, the stronger one may try to reduce the pressure by being emotionally 'unavailable', or by simply leaving. Of course, if the stronger one comes to relish this childlike dependence, then the relationship shades into manipulation.

The dynamics of intimacy

Mutual attention to partner's needs for self-esteem, security, confidence, self-value and so on is the heart and soul of good quality intimacy. Each entices the other into desiring and seeking more intimacy by respecting mutual rights, needs, interests and wishes. They relate to each other in the spirit of 'I'll give to you, if you'll give to me'. Not only must they recognise one another's needs and best interests, they must also be on the same emotional wavelength and be able to identify and respond to feelings appropriately (Goleman 1996). Good communication is essential because 'getting on' with someone also involves understanding meta-messages, gestures and body language. Reading other people psychologically is fundamental to a good relationship.

Of course, such relationships are not trouble free, nor are the partners totally selfless. Some self-interest – like self-protection – is necessary for mental health, because it helps preserve or boost confidence and self-esteem. But, too much self-interest will inevitably turn relationships sour. 'Soft manipulation' strikes the right balance and is an important means by which partners get what they want from each other. However, mutual benign control will evaporate completely if one person begins to rely on 'harder' manipulation.

If the quality of intimacy is poor, partners again focus on each other's identity, needs and feelings, but in a negative and self-interested way. Instead of creating or boosting emotional closeness partners are more concerned with gaining the other's compliance. The game is played according to the maxim 'unless you give to me, I won't give to you'. To achieve this, players may simulate empathy, sympathy and emotional attunement, to make it easier to manipulate and deceive. Thus, what may seem to be 'positive' emotions are, in fact, masks for duplicity, competitiveness and selfishness. Of course, in themselves, manipulation and deception also require subtle communication skills like being able to read other's feelings and intentions. But here, the very same skills that are essential for genuine intimacy are used to create an illusion of sincerity.

Genuine intimacy involves some soft manipulation and 'moderate' self-interest, but when hard manipulation and excessive self-interest come to the fore, real intimacy erodes. One or both partners spend most of their time trying to outwit, or out-manoeuvre the other in a game of win or lose. They could be said to resemble 'control dramas' (Redfield and Adrienne 1995) in which the partners 'steal' one another's energy in order to ward off fear, pain and abandonment.

3
Psycho-Emotional Needs

The types of intimacy outlined in the previous chapter result from the combined efforts of the two individuals who make up any particular couple. The interpersonal dynamics of their day-to-day dealings determines the quality of their intimacy and stamps a distinctive pattern on it. Before they became a couple they were independently formed individuals albeit strongly influenced by their social environments. Accumulated social experiences before getting together shape each of them as a particular kind of person – confident and assured, or shy and diffident, needing constant reassurance or strongly independent. As such they bring to the relationship certain personal qualities and capacities that inevitably influence the sort of intimacy they achieve as a couple. This chapter examines this aspect of individual development and how it impacts on couple intimacy.

As individuals we look to our intimate relationships to provide us with emotional satisfaction. But while personal relationships are often gratifying and fulfilling, they can also create frustration, anxiety and even desperation. Thus intimate relationships are bound up with the question of what it is we want, desire and need from our social and personal lives. How do our most personal relationships enable or prevent us from being satisfied and happy? In this respect the notion of 'psychobiography' indicates the way in which a person accumulates a unique profile of psycho-emotional needs (desires, capacities, dispositions), formed out of their social experiences over time – from early childhood to later adult life. Thus individuals have 'profiles' suggesting variable levels of need in relation to security, self-esteem, love, approval, self-worth and self-respect and so on, and these influence the extent and quality of the intimacy they achieve in partnerships. Understanding intimacy as formed out of the combined influence of relatively independent social domains – psychobiography being one of them – avoids the mistake of determinism by any one set of social factors (as found in discursive, structural or interactive determinism or general social constructionism).

Each person has her or his own unique profile of needs and desires which impacts on their compatibility with partners and friends. If two people are compatible then a mutually satisfying relationship will follow, but if need profiles clash, then it will result in disappointment or dissatisfaction. The matching or mismatching of partner's intimacy needs, desires and feelings can be observed in how well or badly a relationship is faring and also reflects the type of intimacy they share. For example, if partners generally enjoy time together and look forward to each other's company despite the ups and downs that are a natural part of life together, this would indicate 'dynamic intimacy'. If they feel OK but a tad bored with each other this might suggest 'episodic intimacy'. If they wish that things could be different, perhaps as they once were, it may be that their intimacy is 'semi-detached'. If they are constantly bickering and trying to undermine each other in public as well as in private, it may indicate pretence, manipulative or oppressive types of intimacy.

Basic needs, basic feelings

Some authors have suggested that there are 'basic' or 'core' emotional needs that must be satisfied to achieve well-being in mental life (Maslow 1999, Branden 1985). What is meant by 'satisfied' or 'fulfilled' needs some clarification because we each have different requirements. What is 'good' or 'sufficient' for one person may not be so for another. So while it is possible to outline basic or core needs, it is not possible to say with accuracy what any particular individual person wants or needs. For example, while we all require our own 'space', or 'independence' and don't want to be 'suffocated' or overwhelmed by others, we each have different tolerances in this respect. Likewise, humans require some involvement, companionship and friendship, but we all differ in terms of how much of them we need. Further, how we balance needs for independence and togetherness is a personal issue. While some need greater independence, others need more involvement and it's important to bear this in mind in assessing whether partners' needs match up with one another. We must always be aware that there are general basic needs but that individual requirements vary.

Are some core needs more important than others? The short answer to this is no. Precisely because they are fundamental, all core needs tend to clamour for attention at the same time. Of course, there may be times when particular attention has to be paid to a specific need. For example, if a person is going through a trying time, he or she might feel the need for more loving gestures – say for kisses and hugs from their partner. But generally, no one emotional need has more importance than any other. Each core need feeds into and reinforces the others.

It is possible to talk about the psychological need for security, or the need for self-confidence, or the need to feel valued, as if they were independent of each other. Up to a point it's useful to identify and isolate feelings in this way in order to clearly target particular problems or issues. But in the end, mental health and well-being depends on how well the system of core needs fits and works together. Feeling undervalued by a partner or a friend may be a specific problem that needs to be resolved by getting them to be more appreciative and supportive. But being undervalued also adversely affects other feelings – of being loved, of having self-worth, self-respect and so on. As a whole the system of core needs is finely balanced with each need interdependent with the others.

Security and the self

Feeling secure and having good self-esteem are essential for mental health and happiness. They form a basic anchor for other personal attributes and feelings. In everyday life we say things like 'I'm feeling a bit insecure at the moment' or that someone is 'insecure' about their looks. These refer to uncomfortable feelings true enough, but not to life threatening or socially disabling conditions. We often apply such descriptions to people who otherwise feel fairly secure about themselves. But insecurity can be more seriously disabling, interfering with the ability to deal with life and to feel happy. This has been referred to as 'ontological insecurity' (Laing 1969, Giddens 1991, Layder 1997), which involves a cluster of related feelings about personal identity.

The first of these is the feeling of being 'unreal' or phoney in which a person may feel that they are acting a part rather than presenting his or her 'real' self. This may be because they are unhappy with their real self and 'hiding' it by taking on a persona that represents the kind of person she or he wishes to be. Unfortunately, this involves the mental strain of trying to conceal bits of the real self that 'escape' when the individual's guard is down. Along with this sense of falseness an individual might feel unworthy of any of the good things that have happened (or might happen) to them. In comparison to others he or she feels undeserving, insignificant and unimportant.

Personal identity can be negatively impacted by such feelings. For example, insecurity is connected with uncertainty and anxiety, threatening a person's sense of solidity and independence. Serious insecurity typically leads to chronic anxiety, to feelings of meaningless and emptiness and/or that there is no point to life. On the other hand, security is linked with feeling authentic, sincere and genuine, worthy of love, care and attention from others. Security leads to a sense of importance and significance. Thus a person who feels secure also feels respected by others, that his or her opinions are listened to and that others are attracted to them. There is a certainty and clarity about such a person's self-identity which helps create a balance between her or his independence as an individual and the ability to maintain good relationships with others.

But even mild insecurity is bound to affect relationships. Everyone needs to receive overtures and responses that support their sense of security. We must be reassured regularly that we are good, worthy, attractive, useful and valued. If such reassurances and caring responses are absent in an intimate relationship (and it is surprising how often this is so, for one or both partners), then problems will appear in the fabric of the relationship. Resentments and hostilities may be actively expressed. Often, however, they remain unspoken, and in the background, while nevertheless, exerting an unhealthy influence over a relationship.

In some cases a person's insecurities might not be apparent at the start of a relationship and only surface later on. Finding out that a partner (or even a friend) is not the kind of person they first appear to be may create instability in a relationship. If such a person is extremely insecure, they will be difficult to live with because of unpredictable moods or arguments perhaps stemming from excessive possessiveness or jealousy. In serious cases such a person may attempt to restrict his or her partner's freedom in a manipulative and domineering fashion. This often happens in 'manipulative' or 'oppressive' intimacy and it hardly needs to be said that such attempts to be 'in charge' undermine mutual benign control. They almost guarantee the depreciation of trust and intimacy and the withdrawal or holding back of love.

Security and self-esteem

Positive self-esteem is also essential to mental health and, as Branden (1985) suggests, it is about feeling 'competent to live and worthy of

happiness' or 'appropriate to life and to its requirements and challenges'. In this sense self-esteem is an essential foundation for personal
happiness and, like security, it supports personal identity. However, the
strength of security and self-esteem may vary from time to time. For
example, a youngster may be rather insecure, lacking in self-esteem and
appearing shy and awkward, but may become more self-assured and
confident as she or he matures. Likewise, secure adults with good self-
esteem may be suddenly overwhelmed by the loss of a loved one, or by
being made redundant. The resilience of security and self-esteem may
vary according to life circumstances.

But insecurity and self-doubt can also vary in strength and intensity
from moment to moment (Layder 1997). Everyday life itself can pose
many threats to security and self-esteem. At work or at home a person's
judgement may be challenged by a colleague or a partner and eat away at
her or his confidence and sense of competence. They may feel insulted,
put-down, treated inappropriately or badly. An individual may fail in
their efforts to get a job, pass an exam or even win an argument. The
dents in security and self-esteem caused by such incidents can give rise
to embarrassment, humiliation, hurt, anxiety, feelings of worthlessness
and so on. Often such feelings are fleeting, with self-esteem and compo-
sure being restored almost immediately. However, more serious doubts
and uncertainties may set in. In some cases it may be the last straw –
the latest in a long line of such incidents – that finally tips a person
into a chronic state of insecurity and anxiety. Most importantly, a drop
in security or self-esteem will also undermine personal competence and
effectiveness. More generally, a person might feel powerless and unable
to control his or her own life (Gilbert 1992).

Such a scenario could have several consequences for a close relationship. First, someone who is insecure might become over-sensitive and
vulnerable to all manner of real or imagined slights or put-downs from
their partner, who then doesn't know how best to respond. Unless the
situation is properly discussed and dealt with, it may lead to a spiral of
misunderstanding, which just gets worse and worse (Gilbert 1992, Scheff
1990). Second, an insecure person might adopt a 'victim' mentality to
gain sympathy from their partner. But unless a partner is accepting of
and agreeable to this, he or she may feel unfairly 'manipulated' and the
relationship may be damaged.

In these examples the root of the problem is personal ineffectiveness. The more secure partner must try to rebuild the insecure one's
confidence and their ability to use benign influence and control. It
is possible, however, that an insecure person may resort to emotional

blackmail or even physical abuse to compensate for their ineffectiveness. In such cases repairing the relationship would require lengthy and expert, third-party intervention.

Love: The perennial need and desire

There can surely be no dispute about the importance of love for mental well-being but it is important to distinguish between different kinds of love. Perhaps parental love (or that of principal caretaker) is the most crucial kind because the quality of this bond will affect a child's ability to form good loving bonds later in life (Reibstein 1997, Marshall 2006). Where the bond is good a child will, more than likely, be happy and form good loving relationships. Unhappy childhood experiences will lead to a more depressed outlook and either a fear of intimacy itself or an inability to acquire intimacy skills. Although love has several forms including that between friends, neighbours, relatives, it is often assumed that romantic, sexual love provides the most intimate and intense expression of a loving relationship.

Although loving others and being loved by them are crucial, love of self is just as important. Without it the capacity to love others is restricted. If love of others is absent, it is difficult to experience love of the self although loving acceptance of the self is not the same as narcissism. It's more about a caring attitude towards oneself, self-acceptance, integrity and being self-protective when necessary. 'Self-love' in this sense is essential for sustaining self-esteem. Self-hatred or loathing inevitably leads to negativity about one's abilities, competence and worthiness and inevitably undermines security and self-esteem. If a loving self-acceptance is absent, personal happiness and psychological well-being will be elusive. Self-love is crucial because it is the basis for loving others. Self-loathing inhibits positive attitudes towards others.

It would seem obvious that intimate relationships depend on the presence of 'love' between the partners, friends or relatives. It is less obvious that love needs to be 'worked at' regularly for it to remain alive and healthy. All too often people assume that love will take care of itself. But taking love for granted often occurs when intimacy is on the wane – that is, drifting from dynamic intimacy into the episodic or semi-detached types. With the consequent narrowing of self-disclosure that accompanies such a drift, the partners never really ask themselves how they feel towards each other, or discuss the quality of their intimacy. This is not to say that their happiness is not real, or that the relationship is a sham, although, of course, any of these possibilities may also be true. Nevertheless, in the absence of any genuine exploration of their bond, many such people simply 'make-do' and fumble along with a relationship that isn't emotionally fulfilling. One partner may feel short-changed in a rather vague manner, but not moved enough to investigate any further. Alternatively, both partners may secretly feel deeply dissat-isfied and harbour resentments, but never openly express them in their day-to-day lives.

What is missing is a real understanding of what each of them wants and needs emotionally from the relationship. One might need more 'love' than the other – perhaps because they felt deprived as a child. One or both may secretly require more loving responses from their part-ner – demonstrations of affection and care rather than having to simply assume that they are loved. Is an unequal need for love balanced out in other ways? For example, does one partner receive more reassurance over matters of self-esteem, or personal appearance and self-confidence? If there is an imbalance, how do partners feel about it? How do people cope when they need more loving responses?

Another crucial issue concerns the quality of the love between part-ners. If a relationship is to be successful, love must involve not only mutual care and attention, but also respect for each other's freedom, independence and personal growth (Fromm 1971, Rogers 1998, Maslow 1999). However, sometimes this is thwarted by a lack of self-love or self-esteem and is transformed into a constant need for support, atten-tion and ego grooming – which is typical of 'manipulative' intimacy. This raises the question of whether a person has dependency needs that are disguised by the umbrella of love. As with 'oppressive intimacy', the partners may be locked into mutual over-dependence. The question then is, is it possible for them to recognise this and avoid its destructive effects?

Approval and acceptance

As with love, the need for self-approval and approval by others are closely linked. If you don't accept who you are, it will be difficult to accept others. Also, others may misunderstand this as hostility and hold back. Constantly searching for approval in adulthood reflects a child-hood spent seeking, but never finding, parental (or caretaker) approval. Receiving just the right amount is crucial if a child is to move into adulthood with a balanced need for approval. If the balance isn't right, he or she may become trapped in a constant search for approval, fear-ing abandonment or the withdrawal of love and leaving them helpless and desperate. For such a person love is always conditional – on the approval of another. Romantic love is often founded on a mutual search for approval that mirrors partners' unfinished childhood journeys. As long as giving and receiving approval within the partnership are broadly equal, all will be well.

But such arrangements are sensitive and fragile at the best of times and can easily be derailed by events, disagreements and misunderstandings. Imbalances in giving and receiving approval can result from clashes of personality or because of changing needs over time. A person who begins to demand more and more approving responses runs the risk of appearing unsure and ineffective. Over time this may become a burden on the stronger partner. Excessive demands for approval may lead the stronger one to try to carve out more space for himself or herself. Of course, this may simply put increased pressure on the 'needier' partner while simultaneously upping their need for approval. A vicious spiral of depreciating intimacy may develop which is difficult to halt or reverse.

But it's not just excessive approval seeking that may prove trouble-some. Someone who routinely fails to seek the approval of her or his partner can also create a problem. Not seeking approval for things that affect both partners smacks of selfishness, an inflated sense of self-importance, as well as a lack of empathy, care and compassion for a partner. Clearly, someone who doesn't seek their partner's approval over matters of mutual concern will create serious arguments and disagreements. They may even seek to get their way by coercion or intimidation.

Self-worth and self-respect

Feeling intrinsically worthy and that others value you as you value them are strongly linked to security and self-esteem. A person can't experience happiness if she or he feels unworthy and undeserving. The likelihood is that upbeat or happy thoughts and moods will be undermined by the nagging doubt that they are deserved. A person may become so used to this that he or she begins to cling to unhappiness because it feels com-fortable and 'secure', providing them with settled expectations. In fact, being unhappy may have all sorts of hidden pay-offs that an individual may be reluctant to give up (Jeffers 1987). Gaining sympathy, attention, help, support and understanding are major pay-offs. Being unhappy can also let a person off the hook of self-responsibility in general, so that she or he is absolved from making decisions about earning a living or caring for others. It provides a readymade excuse for not taking the initiative in relationship matters, such as giving love and care to a partner, or taking responsibility for emotional issues and making an effort to talk through or resolve such problems.

Intimate relationships strongly influence self-worth and self-respect. As with many emotional issues, lack of self-worth and self-respect may influence relationships in ways that may not be obvious. For example, a partner may privately feel 'put upon' in that they have to shoulder more responsibility for the relationship than seems fair or appropriate. In short, they have to deal with an unhealthy level of dependency from their partner who has largely 'washed their hands' of responsibility. The problem can only be resolved if the 'offending' partner voluntarily acknowledges that he or she has, indeed, become too 'dependent' and that this stems from a lack of self-worth and self-respect. In this respect the partner must also realise that his or her anxiety can only be reduced by taking on more responsibility.

Independence versus involvement

Tension between the need to be alone and the need to be together in relation to a partner can be a perennial source of problems and dissatisfaction within intimate relationships. This is further complicated by the fact that, typically, these needs vary. Some people have a greater general need for independence, while others thrive on the closeness of togetherness. Also in long-term relationships individual's needs may vary at different times. But the needs for independence and togetherness are two sides of the same coin. It is only possible to have a clear view of your own independence by being alone or separate from others and then comparing it with involvement and togetherness.

Moreover, we are social creatures. We depend on others for a vast array of material and psychic comforts including intimate, caring bonds with those special to us. Independence and togetherness are inseparable and fundamental aspects of human existence and personal identity (Layder 1997). It is, therefore, natural for all human beings to need and value them both. But while the tension between them can be positive, it can also raise problems when one partner wants more togetherness while the other prefers independent pursuits. This pattern isn't necessarily because of gender differences (as Tannen 1992, 2002 argues). Upbringing and previous experiences traced in and through their psychobiographies mean that many men value togetherness, while many women crave time for themselves.

Getting the right balance between being together and doing things alone can be difficult, particularly in long-standing relationships. An extreme tendency for partners to favour one side or the other can be linked to engulfment or abandonment anxieties as noted by Miller (1995). Less extreme shifts in such tendencies may occur over time. For instance, one person might increasingly want to do things on his or her own in response to a partner's demand for more attention, company or reassurance, which they find oppressive and stultifying. Regaining a balance in relationships requires both partners' willingness to acknowledge that their behaviours have changed and to talk things through. But because such problems raise sensitive emotional issues, partners are often unwilling to confront them. Instead, they simply become upset or resentful about a partner's behaviour without really knowing why. In this respect they wage a silent war of attrition.

If someone becomes more independent, say going out alone, or pursuing educational studies, or having separate holidays, then a partner might take this as a form of rejection that subsequently impacts on their self-esteem and security, making them even more vulnerable. Handling this without further damage to one another's pride requires the utmost delicacy, trust and sensitivity – all of which might already be in short supply! Certainly, sensitivities may be such that any attempt to confront such issues (even carefully and lovingly) may cause further emotional upset.

Often – although by no means inevitably – a long-standing bond allows greater mutual freedom. For new lovers, being apart, even for a short period of time, can be painful, almost unbearable, whereas for those who have been together for many years, temporary separation may be more easily kept 'in perspective'. Of course, the opposite might also be true. Sometimes long-term partners grow so accustomed to constant companionship that the very thought of being separated causes great stress and anxiety. However, familiarity all too frequently breeds boredom and irritation so that partners increasingly feel the need for time apart in order to keep the relationship going at all. In this scenario both partners silently witness the gradual dissolution of common interests, involvements and activities while at the same time relishing the greater personal space that this allows. At the same time both may remain 'committed' to the relationship – and this is typical of episodic and semi-detached intimacy. This may be workable and satisfactory for both partners although involving a considerable sacrifice of mutual care and involvement.

Unwanted drift

If drifting (as in drifting apart) simply allows partners greater space and independence then it may be 'satisfactory' for both. But many relationships enter into irreversible decline under the (indifferent) noses of the partners. Both may regard it as the end-game in a long and silent (perhaps even bitter) war of attrition. In this sense it represents a kind of 'drifting apart' that developed it own momentum and has come to an inevitable conclusion (typical of the semi-detached, pretence and manipulative intimacy). Tragically, there are also cases in which 'drifting' is unwanted but the partners seem helpless to halt it. This can end up with both partners disillusioned and largely estranged from each other, while remaining puzzled as to why this has happened and why they didn't or couldn't do anything about it. This often occurs because unspoken feelings are not easy to face up to, even if partners are aware of them in the first place. Much of the time 'emotion work' goes on below the level of conscious awareness.

A good balance between independence and togetherness is clearly important to a thriving relationship – although it is often difficult to achieve. An inability to be alone is as unhealthy as an excessive need for togetherness. Becoming too dependent suggests insecurity, anxiety and lack of self-confidence. In 'oppressive' intimacy partners drag each other down because they don't realise the destructive effects of their co-dependence. In 'manipulative' intimacy where there is one 'dependent' partner, responsibility for the relationship largely falls into the hands of the one who is 'depended on'. He or she must decide either to live with the imbalance or to try to 'make' the dependent partner aware of the problem and convince him or her to do something about it.

It is necessary for partners (or friends) to be strong and confident in order to achieve the right balance of respect for one another's boundaries. A healthily independent person is less likely to suffocate or overwhelm a partner with attention and affection or with fears and insecurities. Giving a partner the space and freedom to be whom, or what they want to be, encourages them to do the same in return.

Feeling special and understood

Most people want to 'fit in' with others. They don't want to 'stick out like sore thumbs', as the colloquial phrase has it. This is an important way of integrating with others on the basis of likeness. In effect, it is saying, 'I'm just like you, and you are just like me, and that is what gives us common ground and shared interests'. In a similar fashion many couples try to ensure that they blend together and present a 'united front' to the outside world. But although 'fitting' or 'blending in' with others is essential there is also a contrary need to stand out from the crowd, to feel different and a bit special.

This can present a problem for couples when they have established certain habits and routines of 'relating' to each other. Eventually, they become 'habituated' to each other (Duncombe and Marsden 1995) and, as a result, less thoughtful and caring. The stage of 'getting to know' each other has long since passed and thus much of the 'mystery' of the other has diminished, or at least no longer remains such a mystery. As a consequence, the partners don't look at each other with the freshness and openness that was there at the beginning of their relationship. In short, there is a tendency for one or both partners to 'take the other for granted'. They feel they know the other through and through and can predict their attitudes, opinions and reactions. But this habituated way of looking at a partner also 'downgrades' them. He or she is regarded as completely 'known' and thus no longer as a unique and special individual. In such a case an individual might feel that they don't have to make the same effort to understand their partner as they did originally. Day-to-day they begin to assume they don't have to ask their partner about what pleases them or what they think or feel about certain issues. These things are just 'known' in advance!

One effect of being treated in this way is to begin to feel invisible, insignificant and decidedly unspecial. 'You just take me for granted', 'You never ask me how I'm feeling', 'You don't seem to care like you used to do', 'You don't spend enough time with me' are typical refrains from those who feel that their partner is not giving them the attention that their 'specialness' deserves! By overlooking the qualities that once formed the original basis of attraction the 'magic' disappears from the relationship and with it so does most of the excitement and pleasure of 'discovering' new facets of one another.

For a number of reasons it is very difficult to counteract such tendencies as they happen. First, some 'habituation' is inevitable in all intimate relationships, but especially if two people are living together and sharing their lives in detail. There is a sort of necessary predictability about the routines that partners get into and which serve to make the practical aspects of the relationships workable. It is difficult to preserve the practical advantages that flow from this predictability while also preserving a freshness, openness and curiosity between partners. Beyond this is the indisputable fact that long-term partners inevitably get to know one another very well – perhaps too well! And yet this intimate knowledge may be the very reason why the partners like and trust each other so much in the first place. In other words, it is their mutual familiarity that makes them comfortingly attractive.

But there are hidden penalties associated with this. Chiefly, if a relationship is based on the comforts gained from familiarity and reliability, then both partners must also accept the lower grade of intimacy that goes with them. This is because an individual's unique qualities are naturally dissolved into a taken-for-granted view of each other. The warmth and security that comes from being able to depend on each other becomes more important than individual 'special' qualities. So the hidden penalty is that instead of being loved and regarded as a unique person – whose essence is never thoroughly 'known' – partners are loved precisely because they are reliable and dependable – a comfortable certainty in an uncertain world.

Both partners may tacitly accept (even desire) this kind of security and dependability. However, one (or, bizarrely, even both) may also secretly desire to be loved more deeply and profoundly, and resent the fact that they aren't. But the fact that the desire remains private and unspoken may have a corrosive effect on trust and the sincerity of the partner's feelings – as in a move from 'episodic' to 'semi-detached' intimacy. Ideally, of course, there should be a balance of dependability and specialness. Regarding someone as 'a rock' or knowing him or her 'inside out' is fine up to a point. But it is of paramount importance that the 'specialness' of partners always plays a role in their dealings with, and feelings for, each other. A partner's individuality must never be forgotten if intimacy is to remain fresh and exciting.

Personal growth: Self-actualisation

Personal growth or 'self-actualisation' (as Maslow, 1999, terms it) is closely linked with successful relationships and 'dynamic' intimacy. In such relationships respect and trust is high while the partners support one another's personal growth. Self-actualisation in the context of a close relationship entails allowing partners the freedom to develop optimally and to fulfil their potential as human beings. This ensures the well-being of the individual partners while simultaneously supporting the relationship as a whole. Ideally, mutual growth should lead to greater harmony and integration – an overall strengthening of the bond. However, personal growth frequently alters the balance of power and control causing dissatisfaction with the relationship and pressure for change.

Partners who want things to remain the same may be threatened by the changes personal growth may bring. One person may feel that their 'hold' over their partner may be weakened. This often occurs when a partner takes up educational studies later in life and which usually involves meeting new friends and acquiring skills that increase personal power and confidence. An individual may react fearfully if they are already insecure about themselves or their 'hold' on their partner. The increased self-confidence and personal power of one partner might spell the end for an already shaky relationship. On the other hand, if a relationship is strong enough in the first place, it might be able to readjust. But both partners must be willing and able to deal with the problems posed by such changes.

A serious difficulty may arise if a newly 'empowered' partner is seen as a threat to the benefits enjoyed by someone who was previously in the stronger position. If the 'empowered' partner wants to change things and the 'threatened' partner is chronically insecure, there may be a battle for control in which the threatened and insecure partner may resort to intimidation or even violence – which is often the case in spousal abuse (Horley 2000). Any kind of personal growth forces partners to readjust to new needs, demands and new forms of influence over one another. However, there is no reason why a revamped relationship cannot emerge from the shell of the old one. Relationships must constantly renew themselves to avoid becoming stale with the partners taking each other for granted. Habituation and being 'taken for granted' are, perhaps, the cruellest enemies of intimate relationships.

Intimacy and psycho-emotional needs

It is highly probable that a significant part of an individual's array of psycho-emotional needs is established in early childhood as a result of their interactions with parents and primary caretakers. However, an individual's particular profile continually develops and changes throughout adult life and is derived from their psychobiographical experience of various aspects of the social world and significant others. A person's need profile clusters around core emotions essential for effective participation in the social world such as security, self-esteem, love, approval, acceptance, self-worth, self-respect, independence and togetherness, growth and self-development and so on. Psycho-emotional needs manifest themselves as personal qualities, characteristics and dispositions reflecting a particular individual's fears, insecurities as well as their social and psychological competencies, skills and abilities.

There is a clear relationship between an individual's psycho-emotional profile and intimacy since such needs, desires and predispositions are either satisfied or thwarted through the vehicle of personal relationships. An individual's specific need profile largely determines what she or he can contribute to, and take from, intimate relationships and so, ultimately, the success or failure of couple intimacy depends in good part on the compatibility of these profiles. The matching or mismatching of partners' 'need profiles' influences the quality of intimacy and the type of intimacy problems they will encounter at different points in their relationship. On the one hand, understanding individual psychobiographies in this manner links the discussion (in the previous chapter) about the typology of couple intimacy and variations in the quality and nature of self-disclosure. On the other hand, it connects with the discussion (in the next chapter) of the interpersonal strategies that couples use to (benignly) control and influence each other as they negotiate their intimacy.

4
Intimacy and Interpersonal Control

By using various forms of power and control – via skills of persuasion and influence – couples negotiate their sexual and emotional needs and desires. These negotiations may, in fact, lead to mutually satisfying arrangements, but perhaps just as frequently they may result in relationships fraught with tensions, insecurities and disappointments (Craib 1994). Optimal intimacy – intimacy that is satisfying for both partners – requires the liberal presence of what I call 'mutual benign control'. When this is, indeed, present, the needs, desires and rights of each of the partners are judiciously catered for on a fair and equal basis while, at the same time, naked self-interest and manipulation are minimised. An over-reliance on manipulative strategies tends to corrode and devalue intimacy as can be observed in emotional blackmail, or psychological bullying (Forward and Frazier 1998).

Recognising the difference between benign and manipulative-exploitative control in interpersonal behaviour is crucial to understanding the role of power in intimacy. Sociologists (and others), who tend to identify power (and control) solely with domination, and/or as a social structural or group phenomenon, often overlook this important distinction (Jenkins 1994, Miller 1995, Lukes 2005). Mutual benign control is central to intimacy because it is the mechanism that generates positive emotional energy and feelings of self-efficacy. Individual feelings and the emotional tone of couple relationships are closely associated with the use, withholding or withdrawal of benign control. Thus the way in which interpersonal control is negotiated by couples is crucial for the success or failure of their intimacy.

Intimacy and benign control

Intimate relationships are about satisfying our own and our partner's emotional needs. The best way to make this happen is to influence – and thus exert some control over – other's responses. 'Control' is not simply about making someone do something against their wishes – it's about 'influencing' them in a more positive way. Thus, 'control' and even 'manipulation' may be understood in softer, more compassionate ways which include enticing others do what you want them to do willingly, through influence, persuasion and charm. Good examples are getting someone to 'go out on a date', or trying to impress them in a conversation. Convincing an elderly person of the need to lock up securely at night is 'controlling' or 'manipulative' in so far as they do what we think is 'best' for them, even though they may not realise it at the time.

   Couples (and friends) routinely rely on (intimacy) control games and relationships habits – that is, habitual ways of dealing with each other. Influence is achieved by assuring others that we are right rather than by brow-beating them into agreement or by forcing them into anything. Nevertheless, we subtly manipulate and 'benignly' control them by being sympathetic or caring rather than exploitative. In this sense a person is free to 'resist' your overtures and persuasive powers and, indeed, they may be finally 'won over' only by further persuasion or inducement. This differs greatly from overcoming resistance or reluctance by threats or punishment.

   Mutual benign control continually makes and remakes intimacy, but when it goes wrong, relationships founder and often break down. Successful intimacy allows partners each to get what they want from each other through their combined, 'cooperative' efforts. By contrast, in relationships where partners are unhappy, this is usually because they are at odds with each other and dissatisfied with what are giving to, and receiving from, their relationship. Genuine mutuality is thwarted and there is no longer a balance of needs and support.

Men and women: The same but different

Games of influence and control apply equally to men and women. Regardless of gender people obtain what they want by taking account of other's interests, needs and desires. However, some writers have stressed that men and women differ in their approaches to life and relationships and that this causes confusion and misunderstanding (Tannen 1992, 2002, Baron-Cohen 2004). Also, such writers suggest that because men and women are interested in, and want to get different things out of life, they have a hard time making relationships work. However, an exclusive concentration on gender differences overlooks the many similar things that men and women want and need from intimacy. These include a sense of efficacy based on the ability to benignly control, influence and attract others, to establish and maintain social bonds and so on. The personal strategies and skills of men and women are aimed at producing much the same outcome – influencing, persuading and exerting control over the feelings and responses of others. It may be that men and women tend to use different control strategies in different kinds of social circumstances but these strategies are not exclusive to one gender. We are all in the business of attracting, influencing and controlling others as part of a mutual exchange of wants and needs.

Take, for example, basic psychological needs. Unless a person has enough self-esteem, self-confidence and security, he or she may end up lonely, depressed, resentful and unhappy, regardless of their gender. Similarly, if an individual has enough love and intimacy of the right kind in their life, then they'll feel OK about themselves, enjoy life to the full and assume that nothing will get them down for long. In this respect basic psychological needs like security and self-reliance are the same the world over. Obviously, there are cultural, ethnic and gender differences in people's styles, behaviour and preferences. But differences in style often mask the same basic needs for companionship, love, intimacy, attention, approval, self-esteem, the power to attract, and to be effective in the world.

These aspects of behaviour and psychology underline the similarities between human beings rather than differences based on gender, or culture or ethnicity. Unfortunately, many popular psychology books encourage us to think that men and women want radically different things from life and relationships. Some have even suggested that men and women inhabit different worlds (Gray 1992, Moir and Moir 1999, Pease and Pease 2002). This simply reinforces gender stereotypes by overlooking our shared humanness and masking the uniqueness of individuals. The assumption that the influence of gender is overriding implies that the rich variation in personality and individuality is unimportant.

No one should be reduced to a gender stereotype. The very core of individual uniqueness resides in taking responsibility for our own actions – for 'who' we are, what we want and how we live our lives. Many men cry, are good at expressing their emotions, display sensitivity and so on, while countless women do not 'fit' gender stereotypes.

Everyone has a unique repertoire of interpersonal skills and behaviours concerning how she or he deals, or fails to deal, with intimacy in general. This uniqueness is overlooked if human beings are viewed simply as representations of gender characteristics.

Being effective in relationships

Interpersonal control is common to all relationships: between those that do and don't endure, between men and women, or of the same gender, between those with the same or different sexual habits and practices, and so on. Any human bond is influenced by the power and control that flows from it – even if it doesn't appear that way. In this sense personal power refers to the ability to be *effective* in life. Being effective means getting situations or people to work in one's favour, and respond to one's own needs, wishes and desires.

A person who is unable to do this would be simply overawed or frightened most of the time. He or she wouldn't be able to make decisions or express a point of view. As a result, things would mostly be happening *to* them, rather than she or he being able to make things happen *for* themselves. Such people would feel trapped by life's situations like a bad marriage, or a job they didn't like and as a result they would feel unhappy, helpless and vulnerable. To be effective a person must respond to people and events in ways that allow them to have their own needs and desires taken into account. In this sense individuals need to put their personal power into action in order to be effective in social life.

We all have some personal power (sometimes referred to as 'efficacy'; Branden 1985) – it is what makes us effective human beings. This not only entails physical power, it also refers to the way in which we entice others to listen to us and take us into account by using social skills. Because everyone has a unique psychobiography some individuals have more personal power than others – although this is not fixed for all time. More power can be acquired by learning new skills. Control is the active side of personal power, the way a person puts it to use in her or his life. It's the practical side of power, how individuals actually make things happen. In short, control is the means through which personal effectiveness is put into practice.

Effectiveness is closely bound up with desires, feelings and emotions. If someone thinks or behaves on the assumption that he or she can't do anything about a bad situation – being rejected by a lover, or wanting to change jobs, or to get away from an abusive relationship – they will feel depressed, unhappy, unloved and so on. Such feelings are the natural result of not having control over one's personal life and other people. If, on the other hand, a person feels that they do have some control – that she or he can break away from, or overcome, oppressive relationships – then this will generate self-confidence and self-esteem and, in turn, will give rise to a fair amount of fun and joy.

The sense of 'effectiveness' experienced through the exercise of control leads to satisfaction, elation and other positive feelings. In this sense it reminds the individual that she or he 'is able' or 'has the power' to have their needs and desires fulfilled through their relationships. Knowing this helps individuals develop and retain confidence in personal qualities, abilities and skills. That is, it bolsters how they think of themselves, and thus the image they want to project to others (Goffman, 1971, calls this 'impression management'). For instance, we may like to think of ourselves as, say, interesting conversationalists, good neighbours, helpful friends or caring lovers. Accordingly, we will try to convey this impression to others so that they take it into account and treat us appropriately.

Being able to rely on such personal qualities and attributes creates the self-confidence essential for attracting others. Self-belief seems to stimulate the need in others to keep seeking out our company or to try to get closer to us. It also reinforces their willingness to provide us with the things *we* need, such as love, attention, acceptance and respect. It almost goes without saying that general self-esteem greatly depends on the ability to be effective in social relationships.

Control: A positive energising force

Being effective in personal relationships and using benign control and influence are absolutely necessary for creating and maintaining intimacy. It is therefore of the utmost importance not to confuse benign control with malign (exploitative, manipulative) forms. They are utterly different in style, morality and mode and it is essential to bear this in mind. However, it is a very common mistake to think of control (of any sort) as entirely negative and morally dubious – as if was exclusively associated with competition, manipulation and the suppression of creativity, intuition and spirituality.

As noted in Chapter 2, Miller (1995) makes this mistake in his otherwise insightful study of couple intimacy. However, this misunderstanding of power is widely held and deeply entrenched. For example, James Redfield and Carol Adrienne (1995) perpetuate this kind of misunderstanding when they suggest that human beings unconsciously compete with each other for energy in every encounter to ward off feelings of fear, abandonment, pain and so on, which originally formed in childhood. Our habitual way of gaining attention and stealing energy is by enacting 'control dramas' through which we make up for a deficit of attention, self-esteem and self-worth. These control dramas include intimidating others, being hostile and fault finding, being distant and aloof, or playing the victim. However, by seeking to manipulate or dominate the other's attention we become weak and insecure and cut off from our intuition, creativity and spirituality. In contrast, by surrendering the need to control, we become aligned with mystical and universal energy (1995: 95, 99).

Miller's 'intimate terrorism' and Redfield and Adrienne's 'control dramas' present an unjustifiably pessimistic and sometimes cynical view of human nature that fails to recognise the crucial role of benign control in everyday life. Of course, conflict, power struggles and control dramas do exist, but it is highly misleading to imply that all of social life is like this. It is certainly true that some relationships are based on emotional blackmail, psychological manipulation and so on. There are also many relationships based on other forms of malign power and control, and it might be better if they were eradicated. But the point cannot be to eliminate control in general. Certainly, benign influence is preferable to control based on manipulation, competition and repression. But benign control is also essential to personal effectiveness in social relationships, as well as for good self-esteem, self-worth and self-confidence. Without it, it would be impossible for us to draw out appropriate emotional responses from others.

Benign influence and control is a mutual exchange of psycho-emotional energy, it is not 'stealing' or 'competing' for energy at someone else's expense. Although the exchange of energy involved may not always be equal, it is its 'to and fro', give-and-take nature that makes it distinctive. Rather than struggle, conflict and competition, it is best understood as a process of bonding and rapport that allows everyone to get something out of an encounter (Collins 2005). At times, self-assertiveness such as jockeying for conversational turns (having your say) may, at times, take on a mildly competitive edge, albeit often laced with humour. But, this always occurs against a backdrop of 'give and take' between those involved and cannot be interpreted as 'theft' or a struggle for dominance. In fact, it is part of a collective invigoration in which everyone receives emotional energy (Collins 2005).

Benign influence and control thrives on and stimulates creativity and intuition rather than suppresses them. Consider, for example, trying to persuade your partner to be more outgoing or sociable (even though he or she is reluctant and lacking in confidence), because you think you'll both have more fun together as a result. Doing this in a way that is sensitive to their fears and anxieties, while making them feel supported, requires a good deal of imagination and creativity. Since even the briefest and most perfunctory encounter such as greeting someone in the street not only involves mutual power, control and influence, it also requires creativity and intuition to be successful. Everyday life involves using personal power to make things happen, to engage in the ebb and flow of social encounters. In short, social effectiveness is essential for making relationships 'work' in the interests of all concerned.

Surrendering control means surrendering effectiveness, inner power, skill and competence in social relationships. In this sense benign control is an intrinsic and essential part of social life. Without it we would be unable to attract and sustain social relationships. In so far as it relies on the mutual trust and obligations of those involved, there is also a moral aspect to it (Goffman 1983, Giddens 1987, Rawls 1987). Far from 'stealing' one another's energy, mutual benign control is a process of give and take that strengthens emotional bonds. It is about giving and receiving a mutually satisfying balance of psycho-emotional energy. Benign control is about re-energising one another and reinforcing bonds.

Aspects of control: A two-way process

It is tempting to think of control as the work of one person – who controls another – as if the other is simply 'controlled'. But the point of benign control is to entice, seduce or persuade the other into compliance. A person becomes entrained in another's agenda as a willing and committed participant. He or she is invited to 'come aboard', so to speak, and have an active say in what happens and how things work out. One partner becomes an integral part of the other's vision by becoming committed to the agenda on offer and helping shape its further development. A feedback loop of power, control and influence is thus created.

An example of this would be if one partner is keen on keeping in contact with the friends she or he knew before becoming 'a couple', but the other partner wants to make a radical break with previous links. The process of bargaining might go something like the following. The first partner suggests that keeping in contact with his or her friends will benefit the partnership in two ways. First, by making him or her happy they would be a better person to live with. Second, if given a chance, it would become obvious how valuable and nice these friends really are.

The other partner might respond with 'if you must keep your friends I don't want to be relegated in your affections', or 'its fine for you to keep in touch with your friends, but in return I'll expect you to spend a little more time with my parents'. In this respect he or she shows a willingness to fall in line but only if he or she receives 'something' in return. In so doing the other partner's own agenda is set in motion and is developed as a counterpoint. Thus, whoever initiates a particular agenda through a power play immediately stimulates the other's power, creating a continuous feedback loop.

Control: An ever-changing balance

In benign control the power balance is always changing, tilting first towards one person, then towards the other. It's very rarely completely stable or fixed with one person regularly dominating the other. Such changes may occur because of an agreed division of labour in which one person feels more comfortable dealing with particular issues or situations while the other takes responsibility in other areas where they feel 'powerful'. These agreements may be deliberately arrived at, or emerge naturally, over time. One partner may take charge of arranging outings, going on holiday, or keeping in touch with parents and in-laws, while the other takes the lead in terms of domestic arrangements, keeping things tidy, clean and in good working order. Although practical domestic matters may be a point of conflict, emotional issues are even more fraught. Unresolved issues about initiating sex, or being thoughtful, caring and 'romantic' can lead to unhappiness and frustration. Usually the point of contention is about who *should* be 'taking control' in particular situations.

Sometimes, imbalances of power are the result of differences in personality or temperament, such as one person being timid and shy in company while the other is more outgoing and socially confident. Such differences in power, control and influence vary from situation to situation and generally balance themselves out. But sometimes one partner may take temporary advantage of the other when they happen to be in the ascendancy (perhaps to settle an old score), or more 'innocently', to inject an exciting frisson into the relationship. It may be done knowing that when the situation is reversed, more than likely the other partner will do the same – a kind of tit for tat. However, genuine mutually benign control never becomes frozen into a fixed inequality – ebbs and flows in power and control are essential.

Self-disclosure, feelings and control

Even household chores, arranging holidays or keeping in contact with mutual friends involve intimacy and control games and often reflect deeper emotional issues that remain unspoken. They may, in fact, be a source of loving pleasure and pride that feeds back into the relationship making the bond all the stronger for it. But, if doing the chores is regarded as dull and irritating then this may cause resentment and annoyance. But why should a person experience irritation rather than pleasure? Partly this may be the result of a personal preference, a liking or disliking of certain kinds of tasks. But more than likely a person's feelings (about the task) will be directly related to the current state of the relationship, spotlighting the link between control and emotion. Someone who has negative feelings is expressing dissatisfaction with some aspect of personal control – for example, feeling used, or not valued enough, or feeling upset about unresolved issues. Conversely, tackling household chores in an upbeat manner may reflect an individual's satisfaction with their personal control.

But even emotive issues such as sociability, or affection, are frequently about more than they seem. For example, if one partner complains that the other should make more effort to be sociable, or more demonstrative, then he or she is probably signalling a deeper dissatisfaction with the balance of control and emotion in the relationship. In effect, they are indicating more than that the partner 'should kiss them more often', or that they should say 'I love you' more often. They are expressing a deeper dissatisfaction. Perhaps that she or he needs more space, or to feel more valued, or not to be always responsible for taking more of the initiative in matters of intimacy, including sex. It may even be a coded way of saying 'You don't really turn me on any more!' But crucially, displeasure is not fully revealed and remains unspoken. Unfortunately, the same is often true of more positive feelings. Many people think positive things about their partner but don't actually share them. Potentially, this can be as damaging as having directly negative feelings for a partner.

Why do such feelings often remain unrecognised and not discussed by the partners – as Reibstein (1997), Miller (1995), Marshall (2006) and Craib (1998) have observed? One answer to the question is that many people have difficulty expressing emotions and feelings about personal relationships and thus prefer to avoid the issue altogether. Part of the problem is that such feelings are below 'ordinary awareness', so that we are hardly conscious of their importance (Giddens 1984, Vaitkus 1991). Another factor is that feelings come to us as diffuse sensations that are not easy to pin down or put into words. This is even more difficult if we don't have a vocabulary with which to express them. In this respect it's a whole lot easier just to *feel* sad, or lonely, or hurt than to try to put the experiences into words.

In short, we are frequently unsure about the significance of emotions and how to talk about them and this is reinforced by other factors such as fear and anxiety. Some people are afraid of what particular feelings mean about themselves. For instance, does dissatisfaction indicate a weakness, a form of insecurity, an inability to cope, or an unpalatable desire? Some people are afraid of revealing particular feelings about their partner and would prefer to ignore them. Some are ashamed of feelings such as humiliation or overwhelming love. Yet others are afraid what others, or their partner in particular, will say, think, or do if such feelings are revealed.

Benign but not selfless

Since control, self-disclosure and emotion are so closely intertwined it is perhaps not surprising that they are also entangled with issues about egotism and self-interest. Contrary to many spiritual approaches to the self (Tolle 2005), it is a mistake to equate the ego with total selfishness or to imagine that a modicum of self-interest must always be at odds with a concern about the welfare of others. In this respect the ego functions as a centre of awareness providing us with a sense of 'who we are' as unique personal identities (Branden 1985, Layder 2004a). It allows us to distinguish our experience from others and hence enables us to grasp our relation to them. Thus the ego is an essential aspect of the social self. Without it we would have no clearly defined zone of self-interest and would thus be prone to engulfment anxieties (Laing 1969, Miller 1995). In turn, this would thwart the generation of self-esteem, self-value and self-worth. Furthermore, without these essential anchors of personal identity we would be constantly undermined by others – deliberately or inadvertently – in social encounters.

But the ego's essential and positive aspects are completely overlooked by those who insist that it is only concerned with self-interest, or the denial of other's feelings or interests. In this respect selfish motives and desires will always play some part in benign control and influence, even when other's interests are being taken seriously. Even making a partner happy is driven, to some extent, by anticipating the pleasure gained in so doing. It is impossible to separate out one's own interests from a partner's, or the community's or the neighbours'. In this sense, 'softer' versions of self-interest and manipulation are part of benign control and complement the regular shifts in the balance of power in intimate relationships. These do not add up to major selfishness – the kind that *completely excludes* the interests, wishes and desires of others. Taking partners' (or friends) needs and desires into account is never completely free of selfishness in a minor key. In this sense human behaviour is always an unclear mixture of selfishness and altruism. Similarly, 'unconditional' love is surely very rare – possibly reserved for saints and others who have 'transcended' this worldly life. A person who sacrifices much for love at least anticipates that the 'giving' will be satisfying (if not pleasurable) in some way.

Even idealised versions of romantic love or friendship cannot involve total selflessness, because both partners want to satisfy their own desires and needs. We don't treat our partners completely selflessly, nor do we expect them to behave in such a manner towards us. But we do expect them to take our interests and desires into account as they follow their own. We also assume that if we tell them about our personal needs, they will be willing to at least try to meet them. In this sense, love, romance and friendship are based on *implicit* agreements about what we expect of one another. A relationship based on unrealistic expectations about unconditional love cannot survive for long.

Interpersonal control and intimacy

There are two dominant interconnected themes that flow through the foregoing discussion. They are, first, the idea of the individual as 'a seeker of control-through-influence' in relation to his or her psycho-emotional needs and, second, that the quality of couple intimacy is the emergent outcome of interpersonal negotiation. To say that the individual seeks control-through-influence is not to be confused with the idea of the 'powerful self' (identified by Craib [1998] in the work of Giddens [1991, 1992]). Psychobiographical variations in levels of competence, self-esteem, self-confidence and security and so on mean that the ability to influence and control others also varies from individual to individual. In short, there is no generic 'tranformative capacity' as Giddens (1984) suggests.

In couple intimacy individuals seek to control and influence each other in order to achieve sexual and psycho-emotional satisfaction.

But mutual satisfaction is achieved only if they respect each other's rights and respond sensitively to each other's feelings, needs and desires. In this regard partners' attempts at control-through-influence and persuasion are reflected in constant negotiations around their psycho-emotional needs. Thus mutual benign control is absolutely pivotal to the achievement of mutually satisfying intimacy. Of course, mutual benign control never achieves an ideal state. Elements of selfishness creep into any intimate relationship and, in fact, are a natural part of its ongoing dramatic narrative. However, if manipulative strategies begin to overwhelm a relationship making its power basis more and more inflexible, then eventually mutual satisfaction will be fatally compromised.

5
Gender, Intimacy Styles and Skills

This chapter examines and critically reviews evidence suggesting that there are marked differences in the ways men and women approach intimacy. Among others, Tannen (1992, 2002) and Baron-Cohen (2004) have argued that men and women differ in terms of their respective conversational styles, their ability to talk, listen and empathise and thus to support and encourage personal closeness or intimacy. Clearly, the presence of such abilities and skills is necessary for creating the kind of mutual self-disclosure on which modern intimacy is based (Giddens 1992). So it is important to assess the validity of claims that men and women differ in their capacities for intimacy. The view adopted here is that such claims are questionable on various grounds and I outline two strands of argument in support of this position.

First, the theory of social domains (Layder 1997) that provides the underlying framework of this study points to a number of reasons why understanding couple intimacy in terms of generalised gender differences lacks subtlety and explanatory adequacy. The second strand concerns recent work on language and gender by Cameron (2007) and others (Hyde 2005, Holmes 2006) suggesting that there is little real evidence to support the idea of fundamental differences in the way that men and women use language to communicate. In significant ways both strands overlap and complement each other – particularly in so far as they both call for a more sophisticated approach to the issue. However, there are also some important differences of emphasis, particularly in the way the role of power and control is understood.

Social domains, gender and intimacy

To arrive at a truly comprehensive and, therefore, adequate understanding of couple intimacy it is necessary to view it as embedded in, and influenced by, different, but complementary social domains. Instead of understanding behaviour – in this case, couple intimacy – as the outcome of one main domain (as do many sociological accounts) it is seen as the result of the overlapping influence of several. These are described as follows.

The macro influences of culture and group membership

Intimacy is influenced by cultural factors such as ideas, fashions, values and expectations as they are expressed and represented in books, newspapers, magazines, films, videos, music and so on. Notions and ideas about romantic love, the best ways to please your partner, how to make someone fall in love with you, the rituals of courtship, the dangers and frissons of extra-marital sex, the idea of companionate marriage, the sanctity of commitment, are all represented in various cultural forms and thus are often reflected in the behaviour of those people who have been exposed to them. Similarly, the move from pre-modern intimacy based on external ties of tradition, duty and obligation to the modern form in which the couple is at the centre of a 'pure relationship' (Giddens 1992, Beck and Beck-Gernsheim 1995) is an example of the way in which attitudes towards intimacy are shaped by cultural history.

Often in tandem with these influences are those that derive from membership of, and identification with, various social groupings such as those of gender, class, ethnicity and age. Individuals internalise the values, attitudes and habits (the cultural life) of such groupings (Bourdieu talks about group' 'habitus') and this affects the way they view the social world. They perceive it through the lens of their experience of group affiliation and, as a consequence, it shapes their behaviour. Thus, the fact of being a man or a woman, young or old, working class or middle class, of one ethnicity or another will, in some way, affect a person's attitudes and behaviour. Important here is the power of various groupings in relation to others and whether they are dominant or subordinate. Thus it is often claimed (Cameron 2007) that women (as a group) are subordinate to men (as a group) – I shall return to the connection between structural power, gender and intimacy later in the discussion.

Many sociologists are content to focus on the influences of the above domain (including structural, institutional, cultural and group factors). As a consequence, they tend to view individual social behaviour and social interaction as directly shaped by macro influences like gender. The theory of social domains suggests that the relation between society and individual behaviour is more complex and nuanced than this and that the influences of macro or structural factors are selectively filtered and modified by other equally important social domains. As a result, the behaviour of both individuals and that of couples (dyads) is shaped in a more complex and sophisticated manner.

The influence of social settings

Behaviour and interaction – between couples in particular – takes place in the context of various formal and informal social settings (such as the home, work organisation, on the street, in restaurants and so on), and is significantly influenced by them. Each setting is characterised by a set of social rules, obligations and expectations – sometimes quite explicit and formally defined, sometimes more in the form of unspoken informal agreements – about the kind of behaviour that is appropriate within them. Thus in some situations like coffee bars, pubs or public places certain kinds of intimate behaviour – like passionate kissing or embracing – are generally regarded as inappropriate, while in private they may be actively encouraged or expected. Even the deliberate breaking of such rules gains its force or appeal precisely because of the infraction of the rule. The range of behaviour permitted in, or appropriate to, particular settings is vast. In displays of couple intimacy, different social settings significantly influence (positively or negatively) the kind of behaviour that is deemed appropriate. Mostly, of course, intimacy occurs in informal (often domestic) settings – the most intense forms of intimacy usually taking place behind closed doors.

The influence of situated activity – Interpersonal relations

Behaviour is also filtered and shaped by discrete pockets of interpersonal or face-to-face interaction. Situated activity (in many ways similar to Goffman's 'interaction order') is a domain of influence in its own right, because interpersonal activity has its own relatively independent effects on behaviour: how people relate to each other on an immediate face-to-face basis affects their self-identities, how they feel about each other, how they define their relations with each other and so on. In the case of intimacy we have already examined some of the effects of this domain in terms of the way specific couples develop relationship habits and power games around intimacy (for example, what they talk about and how they talk to one another). Such habits and patterns of control do not result simply from the effects of macro structural factors or the influence of social settings. Whilst being in part influenced by both these factors, interpersonal relations also produce their own 'emergent' behavioural effects from the combined inputs of the individuals involved.

The influence of psychobiography

Again the influence of this domain has already been covered in Chapter 3. However, to complete the overall picture of how the combined influence of different domains shapes social behaviour, it has to be pointed out that individual psychobiographies are also responsible for selectively filtering the effects of the other three domains as they flow downwards (and forwards through time and space). So, for example, the macro structural effects of gender on intimacy are filtered through social settings and interpersonal behaviour and, in the final instance, through individual's psychological preferences, dispositions and so forth acquired through social experience over time. But it is important to stress that the direction of the flow of influence is not simply 'downwards' from macro to micro levels; it also moves in the other direction from micro to macro in a reciprocal fashion. Individual characteristics may shape and modify interpersonal behaviour and, in turn, counteract the constraining effects of social settings and/or group membership. There are no fixed or predetermined directions or flows of influence in the way the domains relate to each other. Particular causal influences are always the result of actual empirical circumstances and, as a general rule, cannot be predicted in advance of knowledge of these circumstances. The combined influences and effects of domains on social behaviour are simultaneous and diffuse.

Thus from the point of view of domain theory, it is inappropriate to think in terms of 'fundamental' gender differences (the macro structural effect of group membership) since any such differences will be continually reshaped and modified by the selective influence of other domains. Thus from the domain theory perspective claims about average gender characteristics, such as Tannen's (1992, 2002) that women are better able to talk about feelings than men, and that they prefer cooperation (over men's competitiveness) or Baron-Cohen's (2004) that men have greater 'systematising' skills while women are better at 'empathy', are over-generalised stereotypes always in danger of giving a misleading or inaccurate picture. For instance, the appropriateness of talking about feelings or the intensity and amount of empathy between intimate partners varies from setting to setting, and also depends on differences in the rhythm and flow of emotional energy in their encounters. Finally, empathy and the quality of intimate talk depend on the personal characteristics of the individual partners as well as possible fluctuations in their moods.

From this sketch of some of the central features of domain theory (see Layder [1997, 1998] for detailed accounts), it is clear that the idea of fundamental gender differences – in this case in intimacy skills and behaviour – is difficult to sustain in any realistic sense. Thus the following discussion of the work of those who propagate such a view will naturally be critical. This critical perspective is supported by the work of Cameron (2007) and others, which provides counter evidence for some of the claims made by those who argue for fundamental gender differences. In this regard Cameron suggests that much behaviour is

> influenced by the roles, relationships, expectations and obligations in a particular context. Although we remain men and women in every context, our roles *as* men and women vary from one situation to another, and our linguistic behaviour reflects that variation.

She goes on to point out that 'sometimes the gender differences which matter most are not differences between women and men, but differences between women and women or men and men' (Cameron 2007: 51). It is clear that in this sense Cameron's views directly support and complement some of the propositions of domain theory, although her comments are based on evidence and arguments that are quite independent of the theory. However, in later parts of the following discussion – particularly where I discuss the question of power and control – my approach takes a distinctly different tack from Cameron (and others) and is, in fact, critical of some of their assumptions.

However, it is important to say that the purpose of the overall discussion is not wholly negative. In a more positive vein, examination of this work reveals some of the possible differences in intimacy style that may prove problematic or supportive of good intimacy. It also enables us to define some of the linguistic and communication skills that are necessary for good intimacy regardless of whether they are possessed and/or used by men or women. The discussion first examines Tannen's claims about fundamental gender differences and then moves on to Baron-Cohen's claims, in each case teasing out the purported implications for couple intimacy.

Men, women and conversational styles

Deborah Tannen suggests that men and women regard personal relationships differently and this is expressed in their conversational styles. Tannen arrives at her overall picture by drawing on her own and others' research on the ways men and women use language in everyday conversation. By stressing their 'involvement' and 'connection' with others,

Tannen contends that women seem more concerned with intimacy. With friends they 'minimize differences, try to reach consensus, and avoid the appearance of superiority which would highlight differences' (1992: 26). Thus women are more interested in making connections with other people. They ask themselves: 'is the other person trying to get closer or pull away?' (p. 38). They also feel that using status is manipulative and unfair. But these preferences *per se* cannot be gender-specific, because there are clearly situations (friendship and some work tasks) in which men need to cooperate with each other, make connections and reach agreement and where any other strategy would be dysfunctional and unnecessarily obstructive for all concerned. Trying to be intimate with someone is a case in point. You cannot be intimate with someone unless you try *to connect* with him or her.

Tannen goes on to claim that men tend to see the world of human relations as hierarchical and so status differences are very important. Independence is the key for men (rather than connection and involvement), 'because a primary means of establishing status is to tell others what to do, and taking orders is a marker of low status' (p. 26). Thus men tend to be competitive, and individualistic, as when they jockey for status in a conversation. They ask themselves: 'is the other person trying to be one up, or put me down? Is he trying to establish a dominant position by getting me to do his bidding?' (p. 38). It is because they see the world as hierarchical that they perceive those who play on connection (women) as deceptive because they 'pretend' that status doesn't exist. But this characterisation of the difference between men and women is more of an exaggerated stereotype than a factual statement based on solid evidence. For instance, Baxter (2005) found that there was as much competition as cooperation amongst a group of girls, that they were no less competitive than boys and that their peer groups were no less hierarchical. Goodwin's (2006) research also indicated that girls' behaviour did not fit with the expectation that boys are more assertive and girls are more supportive. She found ample evidence of girls being directly confrontational and argumentative, by giving orders and arguing.

Tannen contends that the fundamental gender difference she describes can lead to all manner of misunderstandings between men and women. For instance, if a man is asked if he and his wife or partner would like to come to dinner, he may show his 'independence' by accepting the invitation without consulting his wife or partner. From his point of view he's showing that he can make decisions without asking anyone's permission. However, his wife or partner might take this as a rejection of her. She would prefer him to consult her not simply out of courtesy, but because she wants to feel valued and close to him by taking her wishes into account. However, Cameron contests the idea that misunderstandings inevitably occur because of fundamental gender differences. She points out that any exchange between human beings can go awry 'simply because language is not telepathy' (2007: 98) not because they communicate in fundamentally different ways.

Nevertheless, Tannen insists that the above example also highlights the fact that men tend to listen for, and concentrate on, the messages in talk and conversation. Women take much more account of the meta-messages, which comment on the relationship (its emotional 'state of play'). In the previous example, the woman 'hears' the meta-message: 'you are not important enough to me to take your views into account'. The fact that her partner acted without taking her views and feelings into account indicates that there is problem between them. According to Tannen, when the man says 'oh by the way I said we'd go over to the Jones's for dinner tomorrow', he focuses on the 'information' and doesn't hear the negative meta-message. He fails to appreciate that the issue is also one of intimacy, and not simply about facts or information. Again, however, Cameron points out that research evidence does not support Tannen's claims. The idea that men and women have 'a particular problem because they differ systematically in their ways of using language, and that this is a major source of conflict between them, does not stand up to scrutiny' (2007: 98–99).

Tannen goes on to suggest that although all humans need both intimacy (involvement) and independence, women tend to focus on the former and men on the latter. However, the very fact that there are universal human needs for *both* involvement and independence implies that they are present to the same extent in men and women. In fact, Hyde's (2005) 'meta analysis' of studies of gender differences in communicative behaviour does not support Tannen's claims here. Again, the idea of fundamental differences between men and women is eminently disputable. However, if we consider the question from the point of view of individual styles and preferences (regardless of gender), it is highly probable that differences in emphasis on involvement and/or independence might cause tension in couples. Individuals (men and women equally) may find themselves at cross-purposes because they value different things and get what they want in different ways. Individuals who value independence will use status competition to establish their 'involvement' with others. Those who value involvement and solidarity with others will use connection to establish intimacy.

Talk and intimacy

Tannen claims that men more readily use what she refers to as 'report-talk' (giving out information) instead of the 'rapport-talk' (getting closer to each other) favoured by women (Tannen 1992: 77). In conversation women tend to establish connections with others. They emphasise similar experiences and what they have in common with others and are critical of those who try to stand out or appear superior. Again, there seems to be scant evidence for these claims. For example, Hyde (2005) found only tiny (statistically insignificant) differences in assertive and affiliative speech and self-disclosure between men and women. Nevertheless, Tannen goes on to suggest that women feel most at home with 'private' conversation and often approach public situations as if they were private. For men, by contrast, talk is a way of maintaining status and independence in social life. As Tannen says, this is done by exhibiting knowledge and skill, and by holding centre stage through verbal performance such as story-telling, joking or imparting information. Men are comfortable with 'public speaking' in larger groups. They often approach even the most private situations as if they were public by offering a 'report' rather than rapport. However, it is likely, as Cameron says, that such examples of differences in behaviour are influenced by variations in context (such as formal versus informal situations) and the roles, expectations and obligations that are associated with them (Cameron 2007: 119).

Tannen asserts that these differences may also be the cause of misunderstanding and hurt between men and women. For example, while some men are often lively and entertaining 'talkers' at parties or in the company of mutual friends, at home alone with their partners, women often complain that the man with whom they are most intimate 'doesn't talk to me' and 'doesn't listen to me'. However, according to Tannen, often men won't talk about fleeting thoughts and feelings experienced throughout the day (things that a woman might share with close friends), because to him they don't seem important or interesting. What men regard as 'important' (sports, politics, news, current affairs) is usually different from women (thoughts and feelings, who called, who they met, what they said). These characterisations are somewhat contradicted by Hyde's (2005) analysis of a large number of studies which found minimal differences between talkativeness and speech production between males and females.

Nevertheless in Tannen's view, talk, for women, 'is' involvement, and listening shows care and interest. On the other hand, men's taciturnity is perceived as a failure of intimacy: 'He's keeping things from her: he's lost interest in her; he's pulling away' (p. 83). For their part many men don't feel the need for talk – the companionability of their partner's presence is all they need and cherish. They feel that home is a comforting place where they don't need to 'prove themselves through verbal display' and are 'free to remain silent'. For women, on the other hand, 'home is a place where they are free to talk, and where they feel the greatest need for talk, with those they are closest to' (p. 86). However, Tannen is remiss for not considering the possibility that such attitudes and pre-dispositions may derive from a number of factors other than systematic gender differences – for instance, the influence of class or contextual or situational factors, or even simply individual (psychobiographical) preferences.

Differences in listening

All of us want to be understood and valued by others while others are dependent on us to do the same for them. The act of 'listening' to someone is a practical way of showing this. Tannen suggests that because of their different listening skills women may get the impression that men aren't listening to them when they really are. Drawing on the work of Maltz and Borker (1983), Tannen explains that this happens because men have different ways of showing they're listening. In conversations women are more inclined to ask questions and give more listening responses like *mhm, uh-uh* and *yeah*. Also, by agreeing and laughing more, they are generally more enthusiastic and positive. Cameron (2007: 84) points out that Maltz and Borker meant this to be a speculative suggestion – something that may or may not be confirmed by further test and evidence. Unfortunately, Tannen takes it as a statement of evidentially based fact and goes on to suggest that in all these ways women show they are listening and in so doing create rapport and encourage further talk. Men, by contrast, give fewer listening signals. They tend to make statements rather than ask questions, and challenge other speakers rather than agree with them. Such men compete to 'take the floor' in a conversation rather than being part of the 'audience' for another speaker. In conversations men generally want to give out information and opinions rather than be attentive listeners. Again this is somewhat contested by the research by Reid-Thomas (1993) who found that it is context, not gender, which indicates how people should interpret minimal responses.

Tannen uses Maltz and Borker's work to show that not only do women give more listening signals, but also that the signals they give have different meanings for men and women. Women use 'yeah' to mean 'I'm with you' (or 'I'm listening to what you say'), whereas men tend to say 'yeah' only when they agree. This may lead to misunderstandings. If a woman says 'yeah, yeah' as a man speaks to her and then says she doesn't agree with him, he may think that she is being insincere or that she was just saying yeah whilst not really listening. On the other hand, if a man does not say anything while a woman is speaking to him, she may conclude that he's not listening at all. According to Tannen, women are clearly focusing on the meta-messages of talk, while men focus on the message level. However, to reinforce the point made earlier, Cameron points out that Maltz and Borker

> did not carry out systematic tests to see if men and women interpreted the same minimal responses differently. The point of their article was to raise the possibility that a gender difference might exist, and suggest that this should be investigated in future research. But as happens all too frequently with claims about male–female differences, what was put forward as a speculation soon started to be cited as a fact.
>
> (Cameron 2007: 83–4)

Power, indirectness and misunderstandings

In Tannen's view women generally use cooperation to give them power. Men think that power is more about individual competition. For them life is a contest, 'in which they are constantly tested and must perform, in order to avoid the risk of failure' (1992: 178). In addition, for women disagreement implies a threat to intimacy, whereas men regard the expression of disagreement as a sign of intimacy (p. 168). To achieve better communication Tannen suggests that many women 'could learn from men to accept some conflict and difference without seeing it as a threat to intimacy, and many men could learn from women to accept interdependence without seeing it as a threat to their freedom' (p. 294). But such assertions must be judged against Cameron's view that although some conflicts between individual men and women are caused by misunderstanding, 'the research evidence does not support the claims made by Tannen and others about the nature, the causes and prevalence of male–female miscommunication' (2007: 98).

Tannen argues that women are typically indirect when expressing their wishes, wants and needs while men are often more *direct*. For example, a man might ask a woman 'Will you please go to the shop?' whereas a woman might say 'I do need some things, but I'm too tired to go to the shops'. Tannen suggests that women's indirectness is not because they are powerless and don't feel they have the right to ask directly. Rather, being indirect helps to establish connection and rapport by getting others to want the same thing, or offer it freely. Being direct and 'demanding' is about being one-up because others are doing what you tell them (Tannen 1992: 225). But yet again Tannen's claims in this case about women's greater indirectness are not necessarily borne out by the evidence presented by Goodwin (2006) who shows that they rely also on direct strategies.

Yet despite this lack of corroborating evidence, Tannen pushes her thesis even further by suggesting that these purported gender differences can lead to serious misunderstandings. But given that these differences may be minimal or even non-existent it is better to envisage misunderstandings as the result of individual psychobiographical differences. Such individual differences of style may, in fact, set in motion 'a mutually aggravating spiral by which each person's response to the other's behaviour provokes more exaggerated forms of the divergent behaviour'. For example, a person who is afraid of losing his or her freedom will pull away as soon as they think that someone is trying to 'control' them. The other (man or woman) may see this as a threat to intimacy and try to get closer in response. However, this only makes him or her pull away further in fear, which simply increases their fears about intimacy in 'an ever-widening spiral' (Tannen 1992: 282).

Essential intimacy skills

Tannen clearly makes exaggerated claims about fundamental gender differences which may well be better understood as stemming from the selective conditioning effects of different social domains (Layder 1997) or in terms of Cameron's (2007) complementary emphasis on roles, expectations, obligations and contextual variations. But if for the moment we disregard Tannen's more contentious claims about gender differences, it is possible that an examination of some of the issues and topics she focuses on may tell us something about the conversational and communication skills that are essential for intimacy. For example, conversational styles stressing connection, involvement, sharing, affiliation and closeness facilitate intimacy more than those that stress independence, competitiveness and status. Other things reinforce these styles. For example, in 'rapport talk' the talk is an end in itself and contrasts with 'report talk', which may provide a means of 'being one-up' in a conversation. Similarly, to be good at intimacy you must be good at 'listening'. By making supportive comments and sounds, a good listener may encourage another to 'open-up' and talk about personal issues he or she might not otherwise disclose. Where both partners are good listeners, closeness and bonding will follow.

Certainly, being indirect and using 'meta-messages' are not indications of weakness. In fact, they are essential for intimacy. Implying that someone should do something rather than directly asking them to do it gains the pay-off of rapport. Persuading them to volunteer, rather than requiring them to comply, avoids the risk of insulting them. Indirectness is strongly linked with meta-messages in talk. In order to respond to the real underlying message, the recipient must be sensitive enough to 'hear' it in the first place, and experienced enough to know what it means. It also involves emotional skills like appreciating others' feelings and circumstances. Giving off the right signals, and striking the right 'level' of intimacy, is important. Of course, it is possible to be too intimate – too close and too involved – so that a relationship becomes cloying and oppressive. Part of the art of intimacy, therefore, is to help generate a good atmosphere in which self-esteem, self-confidence and self-worth all thrive.

Intimacy, control and influence

Tannen tends to operate with generalised stereotypes when she suggests that women's power is based on their connection and involvement with others whereas men see power very much in individual terms and hence focus on independence and compete for status with others. Tannen overlooks that fact that like all human beings, women as individuals must possess some independence, otherwise they would never be clear or certain about who they were – their personal identity – nor would they be able to generate self-esteem or self-confidence. It may be true that individual women may derive some support from their connection and involvement with others but their own individuality and personal power cannot be completely dependent on it – otherwise they would simply be robotic conformists.

Thus overemphasising women's preference for involvement and connection deflects attention from the fact that they also have individual power, and creates a false contrast with men. The real contrast is in the way individuals (men and women), control and influence others. While they may (perhaps at different times) use different strategies of control and influence, all individuals use their personal power to make things happen. All individuals exercise personal power and control. In this sense women aren't control neutral as Tannen implies. So the real question is how do people (men and women) get they want? How do they enlist the help and support of others to make their lives happen? In this respect indirectness, rapport and involvement are aspects of mutual benign control. It may be that some individuals are more intimacy-friendly because they use benign control more readily than others, but it is still a form of control and influence nevertheless.

Furthermore, Tannen makes a false contrast between getting on with others and the idea of manipulation. But getting on with others requires the use of benign control and 'soft' manipulation. It involves skilfully handling people so that they eventually agree to what you want them to do, while keeping your own self-interests in check. Manipulation is harder and more exploitative when self-interest overrides others' interests, rights and wishes (Layder 2004b). As long as it genuinely embraces another's interest then manipulation remains 'soft'. For example, a person may manipulate (skilfully manage) a partner's feelings and views to make him or her want to start a family or decide to emigrate. Of course, the partner may respond by skilfully persuading them to see or feel otherwise – in short, to change their mind. Longstanding partners often use such 'manipulative' ploys in daily life in relation to both trivial and more serious issues.

Tannen overlooks the importance of interpersonal control (especially in women) because she views it negatively as 'control over' someone (stemming from their status), and thus she believes it to be antithetical to intimacy (closeness). In this sense control is exclusively about making someone do something against her or his will. Thus, Tannen wrongly concludes that control and intimacy (closeness) are quite separate dimensions of social life (2002: 71). But not all control is like this. As we have seen, mutual benign control is an energising force enabling people to get closer by calling out positive emotions in one another. It is both the motive force of intimacy and the glue that bonds people together for mutual benefit. This kind of power and control is about using loving and caring gestures in a persuasive manner to bring out equally loving and caring responses from a partner. In this sense emotions and control are seamlessly interwoven (Layder 2004b). It is clear that negative emotions (pain, frustration, hurt, sadness, hatred, disappointment) often result from dominative or status control. But it is too easily forgotten that mutual benign control generates positive energy and positive emotions (love, care, respect, trust, loyalty). Thus, closeness is brought about through the influence of benign control in satisfying intimacy needs in personal relationships. On the other hand, emotional distance – or impersonality – is about denying intimacy needs through dominative control (and hard manipulation).

By understanding power as a fixed status hierarchy, Tannen fails to capture the multitude of 'informal' ways in which individuals actually use benign power. In this respect mutually satisfying intimacy is created through force of personality, charisma, emotional intelligence (Goleman 1996), personal appeals, seduction, persuasiveness and so on. What I call 'dynamic intimacy' reflects the way the balance of power and control shifts back and forth between partners, depending on the issue (finance, dealing with children, in-laws, emotions, feelings), the kind of situation (an accident, an emergency, a routine chore) and the life stage (reaching a certain age, becoming ill, changing one's views and attitudes). Different phases of life and people's emotional responses often result in temporary shifts in the balance of power. This is an essential part of optimal intimacy.

Hierarchical or dominative control is only relevant to personal relationships where the normal shifting balance of power has become relatively fixed so that one person is in permanent control of the relationship. In this case, it is inappropriate to talk of optimal intimacy, since by its very nature intimacy is something mutual and agreed upon. A fixed status hierarchy in which people see themselves as one up, or one down, doesn't capture the flexibility and complexity of intimate relationships.

Empathy and intimacy

Like Tannen, Baron-Cohen's research suggests that there is an 'essential difference' between men and women. He proposes that 'on average females spontaneously empathize to a greater degree than do males', whereas 'on average, males spontaneously systematize to a greater degree than females' (Baron-Cohen 2004: 2–4). Baron-Cohen stresses that he is not talking about all males or all females, just the average female compared to the average male. Thus, he suggests (quite correctly) that 'such group statistics say nothing about individuals' (p. 183), so that we can expect to find individual males being more empathic while some females will be more adept at systematising. There are significant numbers of males and females who have a balance of empathic and systematising skills. The fact that Baron-Cohen is clearly aware that 'group statistics tell us nothing about individuals' would lead one to think that he would avoid making rather global statements about gender differences. However, despite this, his book is replete with references to gender stereotypes such as men are natural systematisers while women are natural empathisers, or that men and women are suited to particular occupations because of their inherent skills (see Cameron 2007: 6–7).

Because Baron-Cohen also depends on many of the same sources as Tannen (including Tannen herself) for support and confirmation of his own ideas, many of his arguments and statements are subject to the same criticisms.

For instance, Baron-Cohen endorses a number of Tannen's general points. For example, women tend to value connection and involvement while men value power, politics and competition. Women focus more on emotion and while they are capable of aggression at times, it tends to be indirect or covert – such as gossip, exclusion and bitchy remarks. Male aggression is far more direct (pushing, punching, hitting and so on). Importantly, indirect aggression requires greater 'mind reading' skills than does the more direct kind. The male concern with dominance is associated with lower empathising skills. Men attain rank either by being aggressive or 'nasty' to others or by being 'good at an activity; to be expert, knowledgeable and skilled in a particular system' – although both routes involve competition (2004: 42). Females tend to use 'flattery, charm, appreciation and respect' (2004: 44). More generally, females take more notice of the emotional state of others with a view to creating closeness. Males are more self-centred and concerned about protecting their status and its benefits. As mentioned in relation to Tannen, all these assumptions are questionable in the light of the evidence provided by Hyde (2005), Goodwin (2006) and Cameron (2007) herself.

Baron-Cohen goes on to say that 'differences in speech styles suggest that there are key differences in how self- and other-centred each sex is. The speech styles of each sex suggest that there are sex differences in how much speakers set aside their own desires to consider sensitively someone else's. Empathy again' (2004: 56). But if we take seriously the sorts of evidence that Cameron brings to bear against the idea of there being systematic differences between men and women then we must also question the idea of there being differences in 'how self- and other-centred each sex is'. However, if we conceive of speech styles as resulting from an individual's psychobiographical experiences (be they male or female), rather than because of some necessity of their gender, then they could reflect differences in how self- or other-centred different individuals are. Of course, this would have implications for intimacy in the sense that only those individuals who are both self- and other-centred in a fairly balanced manner are capable of true intimacy and empathy.

Baron-Cohen also suggests that 'females are both better empathizers and better in many aspects of language use' (2004: 62) and that female superiority in these language skills 'may be part and parcel of developing good empathising skills. Language skills (including good verbal memory), are essential in seamless chatting and establishing intimacy, to make interaction smooth, fluent and socially binding' (2004: 61). Again, given the questionable nature of the evidence for any demonstrated superiority in language skills (Hyde 2005, Cameron 2007), the idea that being female *per se* entails a greater capacity for empathy is equally suspect. Of course, as with the question of being 'self- or other-centred', if we are talking about differences between individuals, then that is another matter. If one partner (man or woman) is better at empathy then, of course, this will make for an imbalance in intimacy skills.

Empathising versus systematising

Leaving aside the problematic and contestable issue of whether women are better at empathising and men at systematising, Baron-Cohen does manage to vividly characterise what is involved in these two kinds of skills. For Baron-Cohen empathising

> is about spontaneously and naturally tuning into the other person's thoughts and feelings whatever these might be. It is not about reacting to a small number of emotions in others, such as their pain or sadness; it about reading the emotional atmosphere between people. It is about effortlessly putting yourself into another's shoes, sensitively negotiating an interaction with another person so as not to hurt or offend them in any way, caring about another's feelings.
>
> (2004: 24)

A natural empathiser notices other people's feelings and constantly monitors others' tones of voice, their facial expressions (their eyes in particular) to figure out what they're thinking and feeling. An empathiser also continually thinks about what the other person may be thinking, not because they want to manipulate them but because they care about what the other is feeling. She or he wants to comfort others, to make them feel good and protect them from hurt.

Empathy is necessary for real communication; it is the opposite of a monologue or 'talking at' someone. A conversation is not 'story telling, or lecturing, or indoctrinating, or persuading, or dominating or filling silence'. Instead, a true conversation requires empathy which 'allows for a reciprocal dialogue, because you are constantly making space in the conversation for the other person through turn-taking. Empathy allows you to adjust your conversation to be attuned to theirs.' Empathy is essential for social interaction and social relationships. It motives you to care about others' problems and their experiences, to make them feel supported, 'rather than simply offloading your own difficulties onto them' (2004: 25–7).

On the other hand, according to Baron-Cohen, systematising is the 'drive to analyse, explore and construct a system' (2004: 3). It involves figuring out how things work or what the underlying rules are which govern the behaviour of the system. Systems take in phenomena as broad ranging as machines, music, military strategy, the climate, sailing, horticulture, computer programming, libraries, taxonomies, board games, sports, economics, maths, physics, chemistry, logic. The motivation for systematising derives from the desire to understand the system itself. The 'reward' or 'buzz' or 'payoff' comes in discovering the causes of things because this gives you control over the world (2004: 68).

How do empathising and systematising affect intimacy? Baron-Cohen is crystal clear: 'systematizing gets you almost nowhere in most day-to-day social interaction'. This is because 'our behaviour and emotions are not governed by rules to any useful degree' and systematising 'cannot get a foothold into things like a person's fluctuating feelings' and there are no 'simple laws of how people will behave'. In short, 'the natural way to understand and predict the nature of events and objects is to systematise' and for this you need detachment 'in order to monitor information and track which factors cause information to vary'. On the other hand, 'the natural way to understand a person is to empathize' and for this you need some degree of attachment 'in order to recognize that you are interacting with a person, not an object, but a person with feelings, and whose feelings affect your own' (2004: 5). Empathising doesn't obey laws and isn't exact because you can't always be sure that you've made a mental connection with someone.

Clearly, the ability to systematise does not help in the negotiation of social or personal life. Only empathy enables one to do that. If you are predominantly a systematiser then you are surely faced with some difficulties. In very extreme cases of what Baron-Cohen calls the 'extreme male brain', individuals who seem to have only systematising skills are likely to suffer from autism and asperger syndrome. For these individuals, Baron-Cohen offers ample evidence of the damaging effects of extreme systematising on social skills and the general ability to deal with the most commonplace of social rituals, routines and encounters. He devotes a whole chapter to describing the sorts of problems experienced by people who are extremely high systematisers and who are also highly intelligent and successful.

Now while Baron-Cohen provides vivid depictions of both empathising and systematising skills, we must take care to avoid the stereotype characterisations of women as 'natural empathisers' and men as 'natural systematisers'. This is especially important in the light of some of the evidence counter to Tannen's (and others) work. It is surely more plausible to suppose that all human beings need some of both skills depending on what they are doing and the social circumstances in which they are doing it. For instance, the technical aspects of flying an aircraft require an abundance of systematising skills, but when talking to colleagues such as flight crew or passengers – when they need to employ social skills – pilots need to display empathy in no small measure (especially if they are trying to keep passengers calm during an emergency). Likewise, systematising skills are involved in the technical aspects of playing board games, but the interchanges between the game players during the game are also social in nature and rely a good deal on empathic skills. The social nature of the activity in conjunction with the social circumstances in which it occurs are the key features that both require and determine displays of empathy or systematising – not some essential gender or brain sex difference. Sure enough, some individuals may be more proficient in, or at ease with, certain tasks and skills. But social life inherently demands both kinds of skills.

In fact, some of Baron-Cohen's own arguments seem to acknowledge this and undercut the idea of essential differences between men and women. For example, when he says that empathy is 'the glue of social relationships' and that systematising gets you almost nowhere in most day-to-day social interaction or the negotiation of personal life, Baron-Cohen seems to acknowledge that empathy is an intrinsic requirement of social life in all its aspects. Also when describing the mathematician Richard Borcherds, an extreme systemiser, Baron-Cohen remarks that an ordinary friendly conversation was too much for him because he couldn't make sense of the 'hidden meanings' behind 'glances and smiles, of innuendo and double-entendre, of bluff and deception, embarrassment and camouflaged flirtation' (2004: 155–8).

Without doubt, Borcherds faced the particular difficulty that he totally lacked understanding of these social exchanges. But these are by no means restricted to those individuals who have extreme problems in this regard. The ambiguity of such messages, and the subtle games of deniability that frequently surround them, means that it is difficult for *anyone* to be absolutely certain about their meaning – let alone those who are manifestly deficient in empathic skills. If it is true, as I think it is, that people generally experience encounters as a 'fast moving blur of misunderstanding, error, folly and alienation, with only rare and too brief moments of attunement' (Scheff 1990: 50) then most people find some aspects of social life difficult to decipher because of their ambiguous nature. For example, who hasn't experienced the uncertainty of not knowing what a glance or a smile really meant? Who hasn't, at times, been wrong about the meaning of an innuendo or a double-entendre? Who has never been taken in by a bluff or a deception? Who hasn't, at least occasionally, misconstrued an apparent flirtation? Indirect communication of this kind is vague and ambiguous and, therefore, sometimes difficult to fathom.

Conclusion: Gender and couple intimacy

It would seem entirely questionable that the behavioural and psychological differences between the individuals who make up couples are simply the result of fundamental or essential gender differences. As we have seen, gender influences are often indirect and the result of variations in roles, expectations, obligations and contextual variations, as is suggested by both the theory of social domains (Layder 1997) and the research evidence presented by Cameron (2007). The most important differences in couples are those *between individuals*. If individuals habitually use different styles of communication then they will be pulled in rather different directions when it comes to intimacy. Some individuals are locked into competitiveness, status-mindedness and 'independence', have poor listening skills and use conversations primarily to impart information about themselves rather than to get closer to others. Such people are concerned more with how systems work than with feelings and are not equipped to deal with the subtleties and ambiguities of 'good' intimacy. On the other hand, some individuals may tend to focus on connection, sharing and involvement with others – although they may use systematising skills and strategies in other circumstances. Such people are generally good, supportive listeners and encourage others to open up emotionally. They are strong on empathy and rely heavily on 'indirectness', particularly in the use of meta-messages. They tend to use talk to establish and maintain rapport with others.

Tannen characterises these differences as a clash of conversational styles while Baron-Cohen sees them as an expression of greater systematising skills versus better empathic skills. It is important to appreciate that such differences may cause intimacy problems and misunderstandings *between individuals*. But both Tannen's and Baron-Cohen's assumptions that these are expressions of essential or fundamental gender differences has been strongly contested. Moreover, potential clashes are not simply defined through differing styles or skills. Both Tannen and Baron-Cohen overlook the effects of interpersonal control and influence – the different ways in which individuals (men and women) try to get their intimacy needs satisfied through personal relationships.

In this respect benign control is more intimacy-friendly because it trades on, and creates, closeness, connection and rapport, which, in turn, rely on empathy and involvement. It is precisely because these skills are also essential for mutually satisfying intimacy that we must conclude that if partners approach one another in very different ways, it is likely to lead to conflict or arguments and end in resentment and frustration. The most successful couple intimacy will be in relationships in which the partners use benign influence and control on a roughly equal basis. As the theory of social domains bears out, individuals are not gender stereotypes and should not be regarded as such. One of the great dangers of thinking about 'fundamental' or 'essential' gender influences is that it can easily lead to the false assumption that all women are inherently better at intimacy than men. Such assumptions ignore the fact that all human beings are the product of diverse experiences and influences, which result in unique mixtures of personal powers and skills. Thus there are many individuals (including women) who are very competitive and for whom status matters a great deal, while many others (including men) who use benign control and influence and are good at intimacy. Another possibility, perhaps more common than supposed, is that there are partnerships in which individuals who are not at all competitive about status are, nonetheless, not particularly good at intimacy. These people find it difficult to talk about their own or other's feelings.

In this sense it is important to distinguish between different aspects of intimacy. To create good intimacy it helps if a person values connection and involvement with others. But this in itself is not enough. The same is true of empathy, which is perhaps even more important for good intimacy. For good intimacy to thrive both partners must be capable of communicating freely about one another's deepest feelings. Self-disclosure demands the ability to speak about things that may in fact be difficult to address and which require some insight and sensitivity, not to say a great effort of will. But if the partners are not capable of this – or one of them is not – then they will struggle to achieve full and lasting intimacy.

6
Arguments, Indirectness and Non-Disclosure

Following on from the idea that individuals' personal styles and skills affect the quality of intimacy, this chapter explores the possible impact of such differences on the day-to-day experiences of couples as they negotiate their intimacy needs with one another. It examines the question of whether (and how) different conflict styles impact on the quality of mutual self-disclosure between couples. As we have already noted at a number of junctures, self-disclosure is at the heart of modern intimacy – in the form of the pure relationship (Giddens 1992, Beck and Beck-Gernsheim 1995). In particular the chapter focuses on differences between direct and indirect styles of communication in individual partners and how this is reflected in their conflict styles and arguments. Overall, it is suggested that an over-reliance on indirectness in one or both partners can lead to the narrowing down or even disappearance of self-disclosure between partners, which, in turn, may lead to relationship problems with varying degrees of seriousness.

As pointed out in previous chapters, individual partners often adopt rather different strategies of control and influence when it comes to obtaining their needs and desires. So although they may be agreed that intimacy is ultimately about creating love, respect, personal significance and so on, the partners may be far from harmonised when it comes to the methods (of power, control and influence) they use to achieve these ends. Does this mean that they are on a continual collision course as far as expressing themselves and understanding one another's needs are concerned? Does it mean that many couples are doomed to communication failure and an impoverishment of intimacy, care and understanding? Are they destined to misunderstand and talk past one another?

Indirectness and emotion in intimacy

An important issue here is what is meant by indirectness when couples communicate with one another. Cameron (2007: 84–9) has discussed the question of directness in relation to gender. In this respect I agree that there is little evidence to suggest that there are any large or fundamental differences between men and women in terms of their use of indirectness, or in their responses to it. This is important for Cameron who takes issue with claims that women tend to use indirectness more, while men have greater difficulty in understanding indirect communication. Such issues take on monumental importance in the case of rape trials where victims may be (falsely) thought to be both lacking in assertiveness and being unclear that they are not consenting to sex. This complicated issue raises a number of other questions that are not relevant to the immediate discussion. What I would say is that 'indirectness' in human communication is not simply linked to a single issue or problem (like accusations of rape) nor associated with straightforward answers or 'solutions'. It is not clear that Cameron acknowledges that the question of indirectness is complex and multi-faceted. For present purposes, while I agree that men neither use indirectness less, nor are no more confused by it than women, I strongly disagree with the implication that it is never the cause of confusion and miscommunication between couples. Whether or not indirectness is confusing or leads to misunderstandings between intimate partners depends very much on the exact context in which it occurs, as well as the emotional content (and meaning) of the message or information being conveyed.

Cameron discusses only four examples of indirectness. Three of them are about mundane practical matters which Cameron herself regards as 'petty', while the other concerns the 'just say no' debate about rape and sexual assault. The first three stem originally from Gray's (1992) work in which he gives the example of 'the groceries are in the car' as an indirect request which really means 'bring the groceries in'. A variant on this would be saying 'could you bring in the groceries' or 'could you empty the trash' (rather than the more direct 'would you bring in the groceries' or 'would you empty the trash'). Cameron insists that these sorts of requests are not really indirect or confusing. Depending on the context (that is who is saying what to whom and in what circumstances), some apparent misunderstandings are 'tactical rather than real' and that 'pretending not to understand what someone wants you to do is one way to avoid doing it' (2007: 89). Cameron may well be right in the case of examples like this which are 'petty' (as she describes them; 'fairly incon-sequential' as I would characterise them). Far more is at stake (again as she rightly notes, p. 89) with regard to the other example, of whether women who are subject to sexual assault are being clear about their own wishes.

There is, as Cameron acknowledges, a vast difference between these examples in terms of their practical and emotional implications, but in giving these extreme cases as her only examples of indirectness she over-looks many 'intermediate' ones that play an important role in everyday couple intimacy. The latter concerns issues that are not simply about petty practical matters like emptying the trash, bringing in the gro-ceries or even, fetching ketchup at family dinners (Cameron 2007: 88). On the other hand, neither do they involve serious allegations about criminal assault. First and foremost, the examples I refer to involve matters of emotional import – coded messages about partners' feelings towards each other, the 'state' of their relationship, what they love and cherish about their partner, what they wish they could change about their partner, or their regrets about what cannot be changed in the relationship. Such issues are the focus of continuous and routine negoti-ations between partners, sometimes consciously and deliberately – and thus directly. More often, however, they are unintentionally and indi-rectly 'negotiated' through actions (gestures) or even, the *way* things are talked about. That is, such matters are expressed in a verbally indi-rect manner through meta-messages – the hidden messages encoded (or encrypted) in words, actions or gestures – including things left unsaid. It is these everyday, but non-trivial, kinds of indirectness that can have a profound impact on couple intimacy because of the confusion, misunderstandings and tensions that they may cause.

In this respect perhaps the main reason why partners misunderstand one another has to do with the fact that they have different habitual ways of expressing both their own feelings and desires, as well as con-veying what they need from their partners. One person may prefer, or rely on, 'indirectness' in communication, whereas the other might 'tune into', and more readily respond to, directness. For instance, one partner might say 'do you want to go out tonight?' even if it is they themselves who really want this to happen but also want both of them to enjoy the evening. In fact, it may be a coded way of saying 'let's do some-thing together'. However, because one person is listening for a direct message, the other partner may respond 'no I don't really feel like going out', thinking that it is a question about his or her inclinations or pref-erences. Such a person may be completely unaware that, in fact, their partner was saying something about *his or her* own desire for them to do something together. In the event, one person ends up feeling hurt and irritated by the other's rejection of the (indirect) request both for attention and bonding and as a response to this 'insensitivity' may even become difficult and argumentative. The other partner may respond to such 'crotchetiness' by regarding it as 'irrational' moodiness. If the first partner tries to clarify by saying 'well really, I was saying I'd like us to go out tonight – and asking you could we do that?' the other may well respond by saying 'well why didn't you say that, if that's what you meant?' They may go on to think, 'I can't win here, he or she asks me one question, but really means something quite different!'

Crucially, both partners feel misunderstood, hurt and disvalued in the process. But this is not a 'surface' misunderstanding that can be rectified by simply being clearer or by recasting the communication. The problem lies much deeper than this and has to do with the use of different styles and codes of communication. Indirectness trades on a more social, communal style that draws in the other person in order to create rapport or to bond with them. By contrast, directness focuses on the individuality and distinctiveness of the messages being conveyed. One focuses more on the importance of the relationship between those who are communicating, while the other focuses on the informational content of the message itself.

In this sense direct communication is less about establishing a connection with the other than with being specific and explicit about what is being communicated. Directness in this sense is saying what you mean. We cannot conclude from this that one form of communication (directness or indirectness) is 'better' than the other. Rather, it means that the foci and priorities of the speakers are different – one being more concerned with the quality and emotional status of a relationship, while the other focuses on the message itself.

Using meta-messages

Being indirect relies on being able to 'pick up' on what is being said without having to be explicit about it. In the same way, meta-messages comment on the nature and quality of a relationship. In essence, a meta-message is an un-verbalised 'comment' implicit in the message that reveals how well or badly those involved are getting on with one another (Tannen 1992). Strictly, meta-messages represent an added level or layer of meaning compared with indirectness, pure and simple. In the previous example in which one partner asks the other if he or she wants to go out, the problem for the 'receiver' of the message is figuring out what is actually meant. Is it something other than it appears – is it being suggested that they both go out, rather than if she or he wants to go out? However, if we consider the meta-message level, there is a further message in which the initiating partner conveys the hope that they can spend more time together than they have of late. If the other responds by saying 'no I don't feel like going out', the meta-message sent back is that he or she doesn't really care about spending time together. Crucially, at bottom, it means one partner doesn't care enough about the relationship – whether it gets better or worse. In this sense the other doesn't just simply ignore the first partner's 'indirect' desire for them to go out, but is also unable to hear the meta-message that suggests that the relationship is a bit stale and that they both should be making an effort to make the relationship more enjoyable.

In practice being indirect and using meta-messages often go together, as in this example. However, they are distinct in a crucial respect. Indirectness is about saying one thing but really meaning another so the important issue for the 'hearer' is about correctly interpreting the message. Being indirect involves a verbal message even though it is ambiguous. With meta-messages, on the other hand, nothing is explicitly laid out in words. They must, therefore, be grasped intuitively through a deep understanding of a person's feelings or thoughts. Thus, meta-messages are doubly ambiguous. Whereas indirect messages can at least be checked against what is said, there is nothing to compare or measure meta-messages against. Because the meaning is implicit and un-stated, it requires intuitive, empathic understanding. You either get it, and share its meaning with the other person, or you don't. For meta-messages to have any effect those involved must be able to 'get' the message. If one person can't do this then it may result in an almost permanent state of misunderstanding for both partners, as they continually 'talk past' one another.

Emotion and intimacy

One partner's greater reliance on indirectness and meta-messages in communication points to a real problem for intimacy. Both indirectness and meta-messages are linked strongly with the expression of emotion. In this respect they convey comments or requests about closeness. These can be positive such as 'we're not close enough', 'let's get closer', 'I love you' and so on, which celebrate the vibrancy of the bond. But they may also express more negative emotions about the apparent deterioration of a bond such as 'we don't spend enough time doing things together', or 'you think more of your friends than me'. Those who are low on empathy often employ another kind of 'indirectness'. This manifests itself as a refusal to disclose feelings – as in prolonged periods of silence, talking about anything but feelings, emotional withdrawal and so forth. Being indirect in this way is not linked with bonding and intimacy. Rather it is about unexpressed anger, fear, pain, hostility, resentment and bitterness. In a similar manner a preference for 'direct' facts or information largely reflects a suppression of feelings.

This suggests that because such individuals don't generally express their emotions they may be less 'in touch' with feelings of closeness, tenderness, caring, vulnerability and so on. It does seem that a preference for directness suggests a low level of emotional literacy (Goleman 1996). Second, they will find it difficult to empathise with the intimacy requests and needs of others, particularly their partners. If one partner is a typical empathiser who relies on indirectness and meta-messages, while the other is reliant on direct, information-based communication and/or non-disclosure – they are on a collision course. This is because their attempts at exchanging intimacies will be severely hampered.

A closer look at the problem

Clearly, one conclusion that could be drawn from the above discussion is that those who rely more on indirect communication are better at expressing emotion and intimacy. The solution to the problem would thus appear to be quite simple; that those indirect communicators most affected need to be educated in the arts of intimacy and empathy because they need to understand their own and their partner's emotional and intimacy needs. But would this solve the problem? The crux of the issue is whether the assumption that indirectness is a better way of expressing feelings really stands up. It may be true that a facility for indirectness makes a person more 'in touch' with intimate matters, but are they really 'good communicators' of emotion and intimacy? Is their understanding of these issues superior? Is an upgrading of skills all that is required to fill the intimacy vacuum? Would it eradicate misunderstandings and miscommunications?

Indirectness and meta-messages of this type may be intimacy-friendly but they are also inherently vague, opaque and ambiguous. Even when such messages are detected in the first place, their meanings are not straightforward because they can be interpreted in many different ways.

There is no guarantee they will be 'correctly' understood – that is, as the sender intended them to be understood. For those who already have problems with intimacy, dealing with or responding to an intuitive and ambiguous style makes their task doubly difficult. This is because even if they learn to appreciate their partner's efforts at communication, they can only make an untutored guess at what they mean. Of course, it is fairly easy to acquire a smattering of knowledge about non-verbal gestures such as tone of voice, facial expression, eye contact, touch and so on. In this sense a superficial understanding of another's feelings such as anger, distance, disapproval, irritation can be developed in someone who lacks them. But a deeper understanding of someone's feelings and thoughts requires explicit, verbal engagement. Thus, talk and conversation are the means through which we tell, promise, request, implore, flatter, tease and please a partner (Malone 1997) and share all those things that are important to us emotionally. In short, this is how we exchange intimacies and convey our needs to one another.

We can only be absolutely sure that we understand someone's innermost thoughts and feelings by talking and listening closely and sensitively to them. Such things cannot be conveyed implicitly or intuitively. We cannot simply 'intuit' what someone else wants. We may think we can, or that we have a rough idea, but unless we check our preconceptions against their actual, stated needs and wishes, we cannot be sure. And this checking, as we know from experience, often reveals how dreadfully amiss we can be.

The need for mutual readjustments

Intuitive knowledge is unreliable and, thus, inexact. It is surely impractical and unrealistic to expect it, on its own, to properly express emotion and intimacy – even though it is frequently highly valued (ill-advisedly) as a powerful emotional tool. Problems of uncertainty and unreliability will arise even if both speakers continually rely on, and are at ease using, intuition. There are bound to be times when its inexactness and ambiguity prove to be impractical. The problem will be even more acute if one person communicates with a partner who regards intuition as completely alien and who habitually listens for, and responds to, verbal directness. It might be better for those individuals who rely almost entirely on indirectness to make more use of precise and explicit language so that their messages are more easily decipherable.

But being able to translate inchoate feelings into words is not easy. And, although an individual may be more in touch with their emotions, they may not necessarily be able to put feelings into words. Nor might such a person be able to arrange feelings in comparative importance, and view them from a wider perspective. For example, someone may feel 'anger' or 'resentment' towards a partner but be unaware that this is because of a need for more space and/or to avoid a partner's attempts at 'control' (as in 'manipulative' or 'oppressive' intimacy). In fact, one reason why such individuals use intuitive communication may be that they are unsure of what their emotions 'mean'. Their inability to translate feelings into words prevents them from grasping their real meaning. If this is so, then they also require an upgrading of intimacy skills.

To avoid misunderstandings and/or talking 'at cross purposes', those using different styles of communication must adjust to each other. On the one hand, some individuals are chronically adrift from their own and other's inner lives and desperately need better intimacy skills if they are to sustain relationships with partners who are skilled at intimacy. They must learn to recognise their emotions and be able to articulate them, in order to create a mutually satisfying dialogue with partners. On the other hand, some individuals might have better relationships, if they were more verbally direct. This is because, first, if their partners already have few intimacy skills, then being more direct and explicit would aid in conveying their emotions, wishes and desires. It would reduce the amount of blind guesswork about feelings and emotions and thus enhance the quality of their dialogue. Also, these people would understand themselves better because their instinctive, intuitive emotional experience would be enriched. Better self-knowledge would make them better communicators of their own wishes and desires. In turn, this would increase their chances of being understood and having their own intimacy needs met.

To go back to a previous example, if a partner asks 'do you feel like going out for a walk?' instead of saying 'I want us both to spend some time together' – it is highly likely that the other partner will think they are being asked solely about their personal preferences. By being more direct about intuitive feelings and by saying what they really mean, it is harder for the other to ignore, or simply remain unaware of his or her feelings. The more discursive and articulate they are, the more they will have a surer grasp of their own needs. The more explicit a person is, the greater the likelihood that a partner will satisfy her or his intimacy needs.

Personal control and emotional blocking

If partners consistently misunderstand one another, then this may lead to estrangement. Over time, good relationships can turn bad because of long chains of misunderstanding creating resentment, frustration, anger, disappointment or hurt. Such chains make it impossible for partners to empathise and sympathise with each other causing emotional blockage. But emotional blockage also stems from a felt lack of control and influence over others – the ability to make them respond to one's own feelings. Constant misunderstandings mean that partners won't be able to influence one another and thus they will feel helpless and impotent. Being unable to practically impact on a partner may easily give rise to irritation, frustration and anger, blocking positive feelings of love, empathy, rapport and care. Being able to influence, control and impact on one another releases a flow of positive energies and emotions.

This reverses 'conventional wisdom' that control only has a negative effect restricting the expression of intimacy. Such a view confuses mutual control with domination – where one person has permanent control and which is characterised by fear, terror, panic and hostility (Layder 2004b). By contrast, mutual benign control is more balanced and frees up the flow of positive emotional energies. However, when one or both partners feel that they don't have enough control and influence in the relationship it can lead to frustration, disappointment, disillusionment and a deteriorating or mutually unsatisfying bond. This happens when a relationship drifts away from 'dynamic' intimacy towards the 'episodic' and 'semi-detached' styles – perhaps even ending up as pretence intimacy. Emotional dissatisfaction (for one or both partners) and the failure to rectify it through discussions or arguments often result in a sense of impotence, of being unable to effectively influence the relationship. Partners emotionally withdraw from each other – perhaps over an extended period of time (Miller 1995, Perel 2007). They no longer mention certain things or raise problems because they feel it's not worth the effort.

Arguments, conflict and intimacy

As noted in Chapter 3, all humans have intimacy needs such as to be valued, cherished, respected, loved and so on (Maslow 1999, Branden 1985). In a balanced relationship these needs are satisfied through loving gifts, which continually recharge the bond. Of course, even in stable relationships partner's moods and feelings are occasionally disrupted by feelings of frustration. But by trying to get their partner to respond to unmet needs, arguments, spats, disagreements and all manner of resentments and insecurities may surface. Where mutual needs remain unsatisfied, ignored, or even actively denied, anger and/or fear is magnified. Sometimes partners continually bicker, argue and snipe at each other (Pease and Pease 2002, Miller 1995) while their relationship steadily corrodes. In dynamic intimacy arguments help to smooth out the inevitable rough patches that arise from time to time by providing answers to problems. But in many relationships arguments do not offer solutions to partnership problems; they simply become an accepted 'way of relating' to one another.

Direct conflict styles

No matter how harmonious and well-matched partners might seem, from time to time they will disagree. The crucial issue is how well they can deal with or resolve such problems. If both are good at dealing with conflicts and disagreements then the after effects will not linger long. If partners can't do this, conflicts may remain unresolved and cause further problems. Susan Quilliam (2001) has usefully distinguished between 'conflict styles' in personal relationships. Although everyone may potentially use these conflict styles, I suggest that those individuals who tend to rely on indirectness either by not saying what they really mean or by relying on meta-messages will tend to favour what Quilliam calls 'appeasement' and 'low-level attack'. In contrast, those who are more direct and rely on information rather than feelings will favour 'high-level attacks' and 'retreat' as conflict styles.

Those individuals who are brought up to be active and show anger will often favour high-level attacks (Quilliam 2001: 70). Such a person might regale their partner with criticisms, shout, have temper tantrums, and even use verbal (and sometimes physical) violence. He or she may say things like 'how dare you, how can you, I hate you, don't do that'. Such anger stems from fear (about rejection, abandonment, being criticised and so on), and is based on insecurity; thus, unfortunately, the high-level attack does nothing to solve these issues. Rather, it assumes that fighting is the best way to obtain 'individual rights'. High-level attackers view themselves as pitted against a hostile world of competitors (in this case her or his partner). But the high-level attack doesn't draw the other person in, it is an expression of anger and fear, rather than an exchange of feelings or a frank airing of needs.

Thus although erupting with anger may be a relatively safe and even 'useful' way of releasing tension, in the long term it does nothing to ease or solve relationship problems. First, as Quilliam notes, 'it puts your partner on the defensive and by hurting him or her makes retaliation more likely. And if your partner does retaliate, your emotions flare up again and lead you to strike back in turn. No chance of a peaceful settlement' (2001: 71). Perhaps more importantly, there is no chance of meaningful dialogue about the very issues causing the conflict in the first place. If a partner using this conflict style is matched against another who is more empathic and indirect then the scene is set for a never-ending war arising from a lack of genuine communication.

Another conflict style is 'retreat' in which an individual denies their own and others' feelings because they create pressure and pain. He or she withdraws, puts up a wall of silence, avoids interaction and refuses to admit there is a problem or may even just walk out. It is an attempt to avoid the discomfort of anger and fear by not expressing them and is even less helpful than high-level attacks. Avoiding or denying emotions is simply pretending the very problems that are causing pain don't exist. But denial and retreat also arise because the individual doesn't understand his or her emotional needs, fears and insecurities.

Of course, leaving the room might be a useful way of calming down if someone is on the point of explosive anger. It provides important 'time out' to collect thoughts and recompose oneself. However, in the long term retreating doesn't help because the other person is excluded and none of the problems are resolved – thus the relationship remains fragile. The only way for the bond to survive (probably as 'episodic' intimacy) would be for the person to learn how to handle the feelings that can no longer be kept under wraps (2001: 71). Clearly, a man or woman who regularly retreats is shutting off from his or her feelings and emotional needs and creating a void at the heart of the relationship (as in 'semi-detached' and 'pretence' intimacy). The bond will not survive unless both partners make a determined effort to understand and readjust to one another.

Indirect conflict styles

'Appeasement' is another conflict style. When disagreements occur the appeaser gives in and might start apologising, agreeing or letting a partner use them as a doormat. The appeaser is trapped in fear of rejection and doesn't feel worthy enough to assert his or her own needs and desires. Backing off from disagreement and conflict (and thus denying their own feelings) seems to offer the safest solution while preserving the relationship intact. An appeaser may think 'if I give in (he or she) will love me for it. If I argue and make it difficult they will leave'. As Quilliam observes, appeasing a partner will keep the peace, but because this is achieved at the expense of one's own needs it will have one of two consequences over the longer term. Suppressed anger may store up and erupt into worse anger at some future date ensuring further trouble down the line. On the other hand, the appeaser may remain the victim of their own fear, which, in the end, paralyses the ability to be assertive about their own needs and feelings. In time this may transform into hopelessness and despair, depression or physical illness.

Unlike 'retreat', 'appeasement' does not indicate that a person doesn't know his or her own feelings, or what he or she needs from a partner. But fearing rejection the individual suppresses her or his own needs in order to keep a partner 'sweet' (typical in 'episodic' and 'semi-detached' intimacy). The appeaser hopes that unmet needs will (eventually) be met when his or her partner finally figures out what they are – even though these needs are not directly expressed. Such hopes are in vain if he or she is dealing with a partner who only responds to direct, factually based messages. Such a partner doesn't pick up unexpressed resentment about not being properly listened to, or cared about.

Another typically indirect approach to conflict is the 'low-level attack'. This includes nagging, whingeing (complaining), being contemptuous (Pease and Pease 2002) and emotional blackmail (Forward and Frazier 1998). These strategies are fraught with the same sort of difficulties as appeasement – as well as some additional ones. In a sense those who nag, whinge or use emotional blackmail make a definite attempt to get what they want. But instead of asking upfront, they make 'demands' in an unclear and ambiguous way. Also, the fact that these strategies are indirect and 'behind the scenes' makes them inherently mischievous, and harmful for intimacy. In the final analysis such styles are 'selfish' in that they are exclusively about the perpetrator's demands and interests. There is no genuine empathy or rapport since they aren't agreed upon or shared.

Nagging involves rather feeble, indirect requests that are heavily guilt-laden such as 'I don't ask you to do much around here' or 'You never take the garbage out', 'Why don't you pick up your clothes?', 'I spend my weekend working my fingers to the bone to make this place look nice while you just sit there all day watching television'. As Alan and Barbara Pease (2002) point out, 'this kind of nagging is pointless, self-defeating and creates a lose/lose situation. With this approach, nagging becomes a corrosive habit that causes great distress, disharmony, resentment, anger and may easily end with a violent reaction.' The stereotypical nagger feels powerless in life and unable to change her or his life in a direct manner– they are frustrated and stuck.

Like many problems in relationships (such as infidelity, verbal or physical abuse, depression and boredom) nagging results from bad communication or, more accurately, non-communication. One part of the problem is that the nagger doesn't directly express what is behind her or his dissatisfaction and instead focuses on a series of seemingly trivial and unconnected issues. However, sensing hostility behind the nagging, the one who is nagged becomes defensive and pulls away. As a result, communication fails and the situation remains unresolved. If a partner nags at someone who is bad at empathy and expressing feelings, the scene is set for a long chain of miscommunications and the stored up problems they contain. Whatever message she or he is repeatedly attempting to get across isn't recognised. One partner just thinks the other is a nag. The 'hidden' message is not heard and cannot be responded to appropriately. Neither partner understands the other or expresses how they really feel.

'Emotional blackmail' as a conflict style also tends to be indirect. Emotional blackmailers tend to be peacekeepers and shy away from saying what they want for fear of being disliked or rejected. An emotional blackmailer finds a way around the risk of being rejected by asking directly for what she or he wants, and by being careful, deceptive and cloaking her or his intentions. The blackmailer aims to obtain another's compliance by the actual or threatened withdrawal of emotional support (Forward and Frazier 1998, Layder 2004b). By manipulating the victim's emotional weaknesses and making him or her feel guilty, the blackmailer forces them to fit in with his or her personal wishes. Accusations such as 'After all I've done for you', 'I can't believe you're being so selfish about this', 'You'll make me ill if you carry on acting this way', 'I've always looked after you, you can't treat me like this' are all designed to harness the victim's fears, secrets and vulnerabilities and manipulate them for personal gain. But this is all covert – the blackmailer will pretend that she or he is, in fact, the one who is doing favours whilst behind the scenes they are plotting to undermine the victim. The selective use of silence and 'cutting off' provides the victim with a bitter taste of what it would be like to have the blackmailer's love, approval and support permanently withdrawn. The blackmailer might seem affable and supportive but all the time is working secretly to obtain what he or she wants.

In a sense emotional blackmail is distinguishable from other indirect conflict styles. The victim must have enough self-awareness to become caught in the trap of guilt laid by the perpetrator. Emotional blackmail can only be effective if the target is fully connected with his or her emotions in the first place. An individual who is low in empathy is unlikely to be susceptible to emotional manipulation (by a blackmailer) if they are already largely adrift from, or at least uncomfortable about, talking about feelings.

Intimacy and arguments

It would seem that arguments are a common feature of all forms of intimacy – both satisfying and unsatisfying. But are arguments a natural, or even 'necessary', part of an intimate relationship? Or is it possible to have an argument-free relationship? This would depend first on the 'compatibility' or otherwise of the partners and their style of intimacy. Thus win-win style arguments – in which partners acknowledge and listen to one another's needs and talk flexibly about solutions – are a feature of 'dynamic' intimacy. By contrast, with 'episodic', 'semi-detached' and 'pretence' intimacy, the majority, or even all arguments, may be by-passed in order to avoid the intensity of feeling they generate. Both partners may decide that they prefer not to engage in verbal conflict because of the tensions and anxiety it causes. As a consequence they are prepared to accept compromises as far as they are possible.

7
Personal Strategies and Repertoires

According to the theory of social domains, differing psychobiographical experiences and involvements in social life are expressed in an individual's unique personal characteristics and subjective dispositions (attitudes, feelings, ways of doing things). Along with the combined influence of other domains (see Chapters 5 and 12), these differences play an important role in conditioning and reshaping the influences of structural or group factors (like gender, class and ethnicity) on the social behaviour of individuals. Thus, for example, the question of the effects of gender or class on an individual's attitudes, feelings and responses to intimacy is frequently less pivotal than examining the kind or style of upbringing he or she has had, and what intimacy strategies have been most useful during the process. In like fashion the interpersonal domain (what I call 'situated activity') is also an important conditioning influence on intimate relationships. This is because intimacy involves some of the basic interpersonal skills required to handle everyday situations. Thus individual strategies are often chosen or modified in relation to their appropriateness in given situations, and not simply 'assigned' as a consequence of structural or group factors like gender, class or ethnicity (Malone 1997).

Because of crucial pyschobiographical differences, each of us has our favourite ways of 'doing' or 'performing' intimacy. Just as we all have a unique personal style of facial expressions and behaviour, so too we have our favourite intimacy strategies. But the strategies themselves are potentially available to everyone. What makes us distinctive as individuals is how we combine these strategies into a 'performance' style that has our personal stamp. This links with a basic theme of this book – that we benignly influence (and thus control) others so as to further our own desires and purposes (while others do the same with us). But by settling on strategies that suit our own purposes, we also help or hinder others in pursuing their desires and interests. This makes the distinction between benign influence and self-interest unclear. The crucial issue is about *how much* we help or hinder others, because no matter how well intentioned we are, our behaviour will always be in part selfish whenever we tend to focus on our own satisfaction. In this respect strategies and repertoires may be distinguished in terms of whether they are based on benign persuasion and 'soft' manipulation, or on self-interest and exploitation.

Strategies based on benign persuasion and soft manipulation

Creating supporting roles

One way of making someone more willing to see your point of view is to offer them a role that supports your own (Weinstein and Deutschberger 1963). This is best achieved by saying things like 'as you and I both know…', or 'we are so much alike in that respect' which helps establish a common bond and makes the other believe that they share your aims and desires (Malone 1997). Couples say things like 'we think alike' or 'we always seem to know what the other is thinking' and, in so doing, create roles for their partners that are difficult to refuse. A person will tend to go along with someone who does this in order to avoid confrontation or unnecessary fuss. But it can also make someone feel as though they aren't really in control of the situation and are being swept along with the other's agenda.

Good examples of this often occur when couples talk to 'outsiders'. One partner might say 'we don't go out very often, we like to keep ourselves to ourselves' or 'neither of us is particularly domestic, we prefer to eat out' or 'we tend to agree on most things'. In such cases it is difficult for the other partner to break into the flow and express disagreement or just a more individual opinion. It might seem easier to accept the role (image or identity) that has been 'offered' than to risk being seen as either 'difficult' or as a couple who 'washes their dirty linen in public'. Of course, partners are sometimes willingly swept along in this manner because they genuinely feel in touch with each other's thoughts and emotions to such an extent that they regard themselves more as a unit than as separate people (Miller 1995, Perel 2007). Hence willing acceptance becomes an expression of their intimacy. For them showing unity and closeness is more important than expressing individual differences.

However, if intimacy becomes less intense (as in the 'episodic' or 'semi-detached' styles) partners will express their differences even more. This is often because they resent being 'manipulated' into accepting their partner's views of them. Examples of such manipulation can be seen in comments like 'darling, you know you always get upset when you think about work issues', or 'you are a martyr to yourself when it comes to forgiving your "ex" (wife or husband)' or 'why don't you stand up for what you know you deserve'. Of course, both may be keen (and able) to manipulate each other, especially in 'oppressive' or 'pretence' intimacy where negative feelings are covered over by pseudo-closeness.

Personal magnetism

Being 'cute', sexually desirable or beautiful are powerful attractors that may kick start intimacy by providing an initial spark of interest. But usually, initial magnetism is not enough to sustain intimacy over longer periods of time. For this to happen other factors are required. For example, sexual attractiveness might not last longer than an immediate sexual frisson. Staying together may require an extra serving of sensitivity and empathy. Similarly, friends may be initially drawn together because they both like to look 'cool', 'hard', 'demure' or 'exciting'. But if they are to remain friends they must also prove their trustworthiness and dependability. The magnetism of physical attractiveness is powerfully enhanced when it is combined with other things like charm, charisma and confidence. 'Charismatic' figures (Weber 1964) such as those who are, or become, leaders (both good and evil, like Christ or Hitler) or celebrities attract crowds of followers or acolytes. But each one of us, in our own small way, will usually have some 'trait' or skill that can be used to influence others – such as charm, or being good at chatting. Using our most attractive and persuasive features helps energise intimate bonds.

In 'dynamic' intimacy both partners lead with their best 'sides' so that the relationship remains fresh and positively charged. Magnetic appeal is used playfully to invite an equally playful response. But attractors can also be used in a self-serving way to gain the upper hand in a relationship. For instance, charm can be used alongside emotional blackmail or even intimidation (Horley 2000). Conversely, an apparently submissive partner might use their vulnerability and helplessness to wrest control away from a dominant partner. In a similar way the appeal of personal magnetism may change over time. What was once thought of as irresistible charm, or beauty, in a loved one may eventually become irritating or embarrassing, blocking communication and corroding intimacy. This is common in episodic and semi-detached intimacy where the partners are emotionally adrift.

Magnetic seduction

Once personal magnetism is combined with more persuasive skills, it becomes powerfully seductive. Although 'seduction' is most commonly linked with sexual conquest, more generally it connotes the way in which individuals entice, beguile or lure others to go along with their wishes and intentions. In magnetic seduction partners may use personal attractors like charm, or physical attributes such as hypnotic eyes, sexual allure and so forth, along with persuasive ploys like teasing, flattery, humour and promises in order to satisfy their own and their partner's desires. In this sense magnetic seduction can play a role in both benign and more manipulative relationships.

Persuasive seduction

This kind of seduction relies on the sheer power of persuasion (Borg 2004) and frequently occurs in romantic partnerships. Persuasive seduction can occur in many ways – through conversation, 'heart to hearts', hinting, innuendo, 'helpful' suggestions, disguised 'advice', special pleading, imploring, begging, promising, arguing, allaying fears and so on. Examples of this are persuading a partner to do, or agree to, various things – such as to spend more time together, to go to a particular holiday destination, to be more sexually demonstrative, to visit relatives less, or even more commonly, to change particular habits, to be more attentive to the children, to have or not to have children. The same is true of friendships. Efforts to get friends to share a holiday, to go out more or less often, to talk about intimate issues, to share leisure activities, to give up or acquire habits like smoking or drug taking, to decide what to do about the plight of a mutual friend, to be supportive and caring, and so on, are the routine stock in trade of friendships. They are typical issues around which friends negotiate their mutual needs and desires. As such persuasive seduction follows the mutual give and take of control and influence, keeping intimacy alive and dynamic.

Of course, persuasive seduction could be used to manipulate or dominate. But sometimes, unequal power is healthy and necessary. For instance, good parenting depends on controlling and influencing children in their 'best interests' and with genuine loving concern. Thus a parent might convince their child that they should visit an elderly grandparent even if they don't want to (Bernstein 1972). Another example, this time, of what I call 'open-ended' or 'suggestive control', is convincing an elderly parent that it is in his or her best interests to move to a safer neighbourhood, despite their misgivings about so doing (Layder 2004b).

The seduction of the gift

Seduction sometimes involves exchanging gifts. Presents like flowers, jewellery and so on are often used, but far more significant are emotional gifts conveying messages of trust such as caring concern, loving gestures, compliments, support, companionship, flattery, gentle teasing. To be properly effective the recipient must respond appropriately as when a compliment is immediately returned, or a humorous remark is followed by an equally light-hearted response, or when a sympathetic ear is offered to someone else's problems. Gift exchanges like this re-energise bonds by stimulating acceptance or love and boosting self-confidence and self-esteem (Collins 2005). Gift seduction only energises relationships in which there is already mutual care and trust. Indeed, it signifies the presence of mutually satisfying, 'dynamic' intimacy. However, some gift giving can be used in a mischievous and manipulative manner to create obligations in a partner. For example, a person may use love, support, sex and so on in order to buy favour with her or his partner, or to compensate for a mistake, a failing or an accident. Often, such instances of pseudo gift giving occur where there is emotional drift between partners, as in episodic or semi-detached intimacy.

Deep knowledge seduction

This trades on the benign use of intimate knowledge of partner's emotional strengths and weaknesses, their flaws and vulnerabilities, to support the emotional needs of both partners (and others who may be affected). This kind of deep personal knowledge of a partner is built on a history of shared experience and feelings. Partners must be able to open up emotionally and trust each other not to use such intimate knowledge to gain unfair advantage. Such high quality intimacy does not follow from one-night stands, brief encounters in cafes, gyms, planes and trains. Rather it results from lasting bonds in which the partners gradually reveal their inner selves over the course of time. Empathy, rapport and emotional intelligence (Goleman 1996) are essential for this kind of intimacy. Partners must be able to read others' emotions and non-verbal signals such as tone of voice, facial expression, bodily posture, eye contact and so on. Being able to articulate feelings and choosing the 'right' way of expressing intent and desire are also crucial to the success of deep knowledge seduction. This is because it requires the interweaving of both partners' desires and intentions creating psychic support for one another.

Enrolment and people management

While partners are largely unaware of the mutually seductive ploys they use, enrolment and people management are much more deliberate. They are designed to encourage shared understanding and agreement (and also observed in jobs that require 'emotional labour'; Hochschild 1983). Intimacy amongst friends or romantic partners in particular requires the ability to identify one's own and other's emotions and to pick up meta-messages (see Chapters 5 and 6). Also crucial are appropriate listening skills such as leaving adequate 'talk space' in which a partner can 'open-up' emotionally. Ironically, appropriate listening skills also include asking sensitive but probing questions when a partner is confused or reluctant to express their feelings. In some respects these skills mirror those of seduction but there are crucial differences. Benign seduction involves full emotional commitment, whereas in enrolment the emotional bond is much less pronounced. As a result it is frequently found in the 'episodic' and 'semi-detached' styles where sincerity and trust are also reduced. The most extreme examples of this strategy are found in 'pretence', 'manipulative' and 'oppressive' intimacy.

Deals and pacts

People are either willingly drawn into the game of seduction – or, flatly refuse to play – on the basis of shared, but fuzzy, emotional understandings. Deals and pacts, on the other hand, are based on explicit agreements of the kind; 'if I do this for you, then you must do that for me'. They are clear agreements about responsibilities and the rewards that follow from sticking to them. Positive pacts are based on shared understandings that support partners emotionally. For example, who does what and when in terms of house work, childminding, leisure pursuits and socialising. But they may also involve more complex agreements, say, about appropriate ways of dealing with children (being liberal or authoritarian) in order to avoid sending out mixed messages. Partners may agree not to undermine one another in public, or to present a united front when dealing with children, or in-laws. They may even arrive at 'working arrangements' about when and how they will make love.

These are 'positive' deals and pacts in that they only work if the partners desire the same thing. They don't work if they suit only one partner. When a pact has developed over time in a way that supports the partners' security and self-esteem, it has an energising effect on the relationship. Negative pacts, on the other hand, may still be 'supportive' but only in the sense of 'propping up' partners' failings. For example, one partner may turn a blind eye to the other's infidelities because they don't feel strong enough to challenge the situation. Alternatively, they may ignore infidelities because they receive material security or psychic support from being 'known as a couple' and having powerful connections. (The high profile cases of Jeffrey and Mary Archer in the UK and Bill and Hilary Clinton in the USA are good examples of such relationships.) In a sense such partnerships are based largely on mutual 'convenience' with both partners getting something out of the deal, but, of course, as forms of intimacy they are deeply flawed.

Emotion work

In 'dynamic' intimacy partners share responsibility for creating and recreating the emotional heart of their relationship. They take equal turns in caring and loving, making physical and sexual contact, talking about feelings, commitment and about how they can change things for the better. This is the routine 'emotion work' necessary for a relationship to keep ticking over properly. Many intimate relationships slowly (or rapidly) fall apart precisely because one or both partners fail to realise the need for constant emotion work. Relationships and individuals are always changing and developing, requiring the renewal of emotional commitments and responsibilities. Without a balance in emotion work the relationship itself will not be refreshed or recharged. Even if partners are not particularly good at it, their willingness to learn is essential. The slightest backing away from emotion work can wreck the fragile balance on which good intimacy rests. Emotional withdrawal by one partner may precipitate a similar move by the other who may resent being left with the main responsibility for emotion work. This more or less describes what happens when 'dynamic' intimacy gives way to 'episodic' or even 'semi-detached' forms.

A number of possible reasons may account for one partner assuming total responsibility for emotion work. The other partner may lack skills or fail to understand the importance of emotion work. Alternatively, one person may shirk responsibility especially if the other seems willing to shoulder the main burden. The one who takes responsibility, in fact, may not be aware of it until it suddenly occurs to them that their partner never talks about feelings or the future of their relationship. Finally, someone who carries the emotional load in a relationship may do so out of insecurity. By immersing themselves in emotion work they gain a sense of control, which, to an extent, allays their fears that the relationship might fall apart if they don't take on the whole burden. But, of course, by monopolising emotion work they leave little room for their partner to join in.

Once the responsibility for emotion work is out of kilter a relationship becomes increasingly unsatisfying for one or both partners. If one person either takes all or refuses to take any responsibility for emotion work, then the other may eventually begin to resent it and enter into a 'battle for control' (Miller 1995). If both partners are happy with an imbalance in emotion work, it is usually because this conveniently covers over their mutual failings. This happens in 'oppressive' intimacy where partners' co-dependence results from their personal flaws or weaknesses. In such cases partners manipulate each other and preserve themselves through a symbiotic relationship. This signals a shift from 'softer', to more selfish manipulation – where identities are undermined and energy dissipates from the bond.

Strategies based on self-interest, manipulation and exploitation

Emotional rescue

A person may give herself or himself emotionally without realising that their partner isn't willing to do the same. But instead of giving up on the relationship, they decide to forge ahead in the hope that they can 'change' or repair the flaws in the partner. Any inadequacy, such as an over controlling or critical nature, chronic insecurity, social anxiety, an unpredictable temper, can become a 'project' for transformation. However, if the flawed partner doesn't want to change, the relationship itself will come under threat. Another problem is that the 'rescuer' bases their liking and attraction for the inadequate partner not on what they 'are' but what they are capable of becoming. They fall in love with the idea of changing him or her into their 'ideal', rather than accepting them for what they are. They may even settle for a partner who doesn't love them or treats them badly because they believe that they can eventually change them.

Emotional rescuers sometimes seek to rescue obviously 'helpless' partners and, by so doing, convince themselves of their own compassionate and loving nature. In this sense the 'rescuer' may be as inadequate as the person they are rescuing and, as a consequence, they 'negatively' support each other. Of course, unless the flawed partner is actively willing to change, the rescuer must resort to various self-deceptions. Thus they try to convince themselves that they just need a little more time, or that (unlike his or her previous partners) 'you' (the rescuer) will be the one who 'loves them enough to change them' or that you are the only one who really understands the 'real' them (De Angelis 1992). Both the rescuer and the rescued deceive themselves by imaging that intimacy can be sustained in this manner. At best, it may provide negative support; at worst, it may deteriorate into manipulation or dependence. It has been suggested that women use this strategy to rescue 'bad' men (De Angelis 1992). This indeed is a familiar story linked with women abuse (Horley 2000), but there are many men who also attempt to rescue women who are inadequate in some way.

Creating dependency

Based as it is on fear of abandonment, the point of this strategy is to make a partner so dependent that they would never consider leaving the relationship. While the stronger partner adopts the role of 'competent adult' the other is cast in the role of 'dependent child' who 'ought to be' submissive and allow the other to take the main responsibility. By constantly hearing the message that he or she is essentially a vulnerable, fragile person, they do indeed become helpless and dependent. The stronger partner takes them under their wing, so to speak, and 'makes the world safe' for them. The more they are defined as dependent, the more convinced that they indeed are, while the competence and strength of the other is reinforced.

When men do this to women they usually take on the role of father figure or protector. But this is not simply about caring and protecting someone who is vulnerable. The point is also to keep his partner in her place by reminding her that she cannot do without his help in finding her way through the world. He always knows more and therefore 'knows best'. He may regard her as 'irrational' or 'emotional', incapable of dealing with the hard realities of life. If he can convince her that she is indeed better off by bowing to his 'superiority' then she will become dependent. Ultimately of course, much rests on her willingness or refusal to accept (even 'exploit') this position.

By contrast, women who use this strategy on men typically adopt the role of mother or carer. She will try to make herself indispensable – and hence create dependency – by mothering him. She may attempt to run his life, doing things for him, reminding him of what he should be doing, talking in baby talk, scolding, making his favourite food, tidying his possessions and generally taking charge where she thinks he is incompetent. A woman might do this in order to make the man so reliant and dependent that he would never consider breaking up and so remove any insecurities or fears she might have about abandonment. At the same time she obtains more attention, affection and intimacy. However, this might have the inadvertent effect of eroding the man's self-esteem, which, in turn, will undermine his ability to give love. He may also resent being smothered and stifled and hence resist or rebel against her (De Angelis 1992).

Relinquishing power

On the face of it this would seem an odd strategy. It is an attempt to acquire rather meagre and seemingly negative 'advantages' by giving away power. If someone fears their partner's criticisms or disapproval, they may tolerate lack of respect or mistreatment. The unacceptable behaviour is more bearable than the rejection. People who are guilt-ridden or low on self-esteem do this when they allow their partner's wants, desires and general life agenda to snuff out the importance of their own needs and desires. They will often give up their interests, ambitions, hobbies, friends or family members in order to avoid conflict with a partner who doesn't approve of them. The disapproval is driven by insecurity and a need to cut a partner off from previous psychic support since it threatens their own control over the relationship (Horley 2000).

An individual may give away power by trying to become the kind of person their partner ideally wants. Such a person tries to adapt their personality and behaviour so that they fit in with a partner's expectations and desires. But by trying to become their ideal person important parts of self-identity are sacrificed. Finally, a person may relinquish power by giving up on his or her own hopes, desires and dreams in order to help a partner's come to fruition. Giving up jobs, or moving to a different country, relinquishing ambitions are all ways of giving away power in a relationship (although they may also be part of an agreed deal or pact). De Angelis (1992: 51) suggests that some women cover up their excellence and competence 'in order to avoid threatening the man in their life' and 'to make him feel better about himself'. Many such women hide their talents and accomplishments from the men in their lives or they talk about themselves in derogatory terms, put themselves down, or refuse to 'take' compliments in order that the man can feel more 'in charge'. By so doing, these women believe that men will love them more. However, as Angelis points out, this belief is illusory because most men believe 'that a woman who exudes self-confidence is very appealing' (1992: 56).

Psychological attrition

Psychological attrition occurs when intimacy is at its lowest ebb. It involves wearing a partner down as if he or she was an opponent in a war game. The strategy includes criticism, whingeing and nagging, which makes the target feel as though they are constantly being interrogated. They must justify and account for everything they do and say. This slowly undermines their defences and so eventually they cave in to the partner's demands. A person who uses this strategy is insecure about his or her tenuous hold on power and their inability to use benign control effectively. But it does not rely on actual or threatened violence – it is a strategy of last resort borne out of desperation. It is the preferred choice of someone who feels powerless and helpless – who manifestly isn't good at benign control and influence. Nagging and whingeing are conflict styles more typically associated with individuals who rely on indirect forms of communication, often alongside emotional manipulation or emotional blackmail. A person who routinely employs psychological attrition is socially ineffectual and profoundly lacking in the skills normally used to influence and control others.

Phoney seduction

This is a manipulative version of seduction. The victim is drawn in by the 'promise' that their love, care or attention will be returned in kind. But the phoney seducer is only concerned with getting her or his way. Phoney seduction encompasses a wide range of behaviours. At one extreme there is sexual seduction as 'conquest' in which the seducer moves on to another potential 'victim' as soon as sexual gratification has been achieved. Of course, if both partners are fully aware and accept this in the first place, then there is no deception involved.

However, if one person thinks that a 'serious' bond is being initiated, or if the seducer is 'economical with the truth' about her or his intentions, then it is phoney seduction. This is typical of the 'Casanova' or 'womanising' syndrome in men (Giddens 1992), although in the modern era a significant number of women also practise sexual conquest and predation.

At the other end of the scale, phoney seduction can be used to manipulate a partner in an established relationship. This is reflected in the habit of some women who 'act like little girls to get what they want from men' (De Angelis 1992: 68–72). A woman might feign naivety or ignorance so that her man feels smart, or she might pretend to be confused so that she doesn't have to make decisions or take responsibility for her life. These and other ploys – like treating men like daddy and wanting him to rescue her – involve a good measure of self-deception as well as wilful manipulation.

Emotional blackmail

Milder forms of manipulation are commonplace in everyday life. For example, sexual intimacy can be offered to make a partner suppress their anger when you admit you've crashed the car, or forgotten to pass on an important message. These are part of the give and take of close relationships and are present in even the most satisfying intimacy. Emotional blackmail, on the other hand, clearly goes beyond ordinary manipulation 'when it is used repeatedly to coerce us into complying with the blackmailer's demands at the expense of your own wishes and well-being' (Forward and Frazier 1998). An emotional blackmailer is someone close, who threatens – either directly or indirectly – to punish us if we don't do what she or he wants. Because many blackmailers are close to us (like family, friends and colleagues) we prefer to strengthen, rather than break, our bonds with them. Along with fear, obligation and guilt, the target is confused – which makes it difficult to refuse the blackmailer's demands.

Some blackmailers are aggressive, upfront and confrontational whilst others are passive, subtle and manipulate 'behind the scenes', so to speak. However, all blackmailers share a fear of change, rejection or a loss of power and control. As Forward and Frazier observe, blackmailers do not have an explicit aim to destroy their victims:

> Rather, they are people for whom blackmail is the ticket to feeling safe and in charge. No matter how confident they look on the outside, blackmailers are operating out of high degrees of anxiety. But then

they snap their fingers and we jump. For a moment, our blackmailers can feel powerful. Emotional blackmail becomes a defence against feeling hurt and afraid.

(Forward and Frazier 1998: 11)

The emotional blackmailer uses the cloak of intimacy to gain knowledge of the target's innermost secrets and vulnerabilities. They threaten to withhold love and approval so that the target feels that they can only be earned by submission and compliance (Layder 2004b). If, for example, someone regards themselves as generous and caring, the blackmailer might accuse them of selfishness. Comments like 'how could you be so selfish after all I've done for you' create obligation and fear of rejection. However, the more that someone gives in to emotional blackmail, the more their own sense of competence, self worth and self-confidence will be eroded. Forward and Frazier identify four typical guises in which emotional blackmailers operate. 'Punishers' clearly signal what will happen if they do not get their way. 'I'll leave you if you go back to work', 'If you try to divorce me you'll never see the kids again', 'if you marry that man (woman) I'll cut you out of my will' are typical threats made aggressively or subtly with the selective use of 'smouldering silence' (1998: 41). 'Self-punishers' threaten to damage their own health or happiness if the target doesn't comply with comments like 'You make me very depressed when you talk like that', or 'If you leave me I'll kill myself'.

'Sufferers' rely on peddling guilt and blaming the target for their own failures. It is as if they say, 'If you don't do what I want, I will suffer and it will be your fault' – as in the statement 'I might as well stick my head in the oven for all you care'. Finally, 'tantalisers' promise rewards such as money, a promotion, love or acceptance if the victim can deal with a never-ending series of tests involving giving the blackmailer what he or she wants. However, because of strings attached to each lure, promise or incentive it becomes an endless game and an effective means of control over the victim.

Clearly, 'punishers' manipulate emotional vulnerabilities as in 'I'll cut you off from loved ones if you don't do what I say' but they seem to differ from the other three types of blackmailer because they operate from a position of aggression and dominance. 'Sufferers', 'self-punishers' and 'tantalisers' offer themselves as supposed 'victims' of the 'selfish' or insufferable behaviour of others. They elicit the sympathy and support of the real targets by 'guilt-tripping' them, so to speak. Punishers, by contrast, lead with direct and explicit threats while the other three are indirect. They create guilt in the target by presenting themselves as the real victims. Individuals who rely on indirect communication are likely to indulge in these kinds of emotional blackmail since they also require much more subtle manipulation of intimacy skills (see Chapters 5 and 6). The aggressive and confrontational style of 'punishers' is more typical of those who rely on direct communication.

Emotional terrorism/emotional bullying

Emotional terrorism stops just short of full-on physical violence although it is often based on implicit threats of violence and intimidation. Again, the terrorist is inadequate or insecure. And because he or she finds it difficult to trust others they attempt to construct a regime in which a partner lives in constant fear of their unpredictable outbursts. The behaviour of a typical emotional bully or terrorist may not be immediately apparent. At first sight, a 'terrorist' may appear to be warm, gentle and intelligent. However, sooner or later their true nature will show through. In a first-hand account after two months of marriage, one woman's husband revealed himself to be a cold manipulative bully (Stewart 1998). He would fly into unpredictable rages over domestic details (such as claiming she had not matched his socks properly), and blaming her totally for what he claimed were her failings and mistakes. He felt inferior to his wife and therefore wanted to have her 'under his thumb'. His emotional bullying involved 'protracted sulking silences'. Such silent rages, sometimes lasting for two weeks, were a very efficient method of gaining control over the relationship and allaying his fears that she would leave him.

Appeasing and mollifying emotional bullies simply encourages the cycle of bullying to continue whilst also undermining the victim's self-esteem. The terrorist's insecurity and inferiority means that they cannot tolerate the slightest indication that they are not in control of the situation. Their emotional bullying is thus a vain attempt to prevent any loss of control or shift of power in the relationship. In the above case the terrorist's combination of extreme rage and sulking silences was a way of externalising and denying his own failures. The need for control over others born out of inadequacy or personal failure is similar to emotional blackmail, but the terrorist or bully is more of a monster. The inner weaknesses of the blackmailer are used as anchors to which the guilt of their targets may be harnessed, while the personal failings of terrorists are somehow transformed into an aggressive hatred of their victims.

Intimacy strategies and repertoires

Individuals naturally draw from the whole range of strategies outlined in this chapter. Of course, the more partners choose from the benign strategies, the more mutually satisfying and energising will be the intimacy games they play. By contrast, if partners routinely use the more manipulative ones, the more their relationships will be energy-draining and swamped by negative emotions. In this respect, 'strategies' are not the quite the same as the games themselves (outlined in the next two chapters). Strategies are best understood as the particular ways in which people play intimacy games – their individual game styles. Intimacy 'games' themselves are more to do with the rules that influence and define the way in which partners deal with each other – the relationship between them, rather than simply their individual styles.

8
Deficit or Energy-Draining Games

In this and the next chapter I describe some of the most common intimacy games played by couples. While Chapter 9 focuses on 'energising' games, this one concentrates on 'energy-draining' games – the ones that cause most trouble in relationships. By describing them first, it is possible to identify those aspects of a relationship that constantly create problems and issues and stifle the happiness of the partners. By first doing this it is perhaps easier to appreciate how they could be transformed or 'healed'. However, first, it is necessary to understand a little about the differences between these games.

Energising and energy-draining games

Why is it that energising intimacy games sometimes degenerate and become energy draining? In energising games the energy flowing between the partners is always increasing because of the positive effects of their interaction. Each person invests their 'own' energy into the shared 'relationship pool', because the relationship makes them feel at ease, happy and content. As a result their commitment and loyalty to one another is intensified. By combining forces partners increase the overall amount of energy circulating in the relationship and thereby strengthen their bond.

   This can be seen in a very simple example, as when a partner or friend suggests to the other that they do something together like go to the cinema, or for a meal, visit friends, or simply spend time in each other's company. In a relationship that is strong and positive, partners will respond to such a suggestion with excitement, anticipating a satisfying sense of togetherness. As a result they are more than willing to invest their energy and enthusiasm into the joint project. Their positive attitude creates rewarding feelings of euphoria and a wish to repeat the experience. The circulation of energy in such a relationship remains unbroken and continuous. Each encounter further adds to the flow of energy because the partners want to constantly re-invest energy to receive the buzz of connection and bonding (Collins 2005). This continuous circulation of energy means that partners never become *isolated* as energy givers and receivers. Their individual energies remain high because a reservoir of shared energy remains circulating in the bond between them. The unbroken circuit means that energy cannot leak away.

Energy-draining games get started with a disruption of the bond between the partners. The flow of energy in the relationship is broken and each partner becomes drained of enthusiasm. The break may occur for different reasons. It may be caused by a personality incompatibility – for instance, an outward sociable person mismatched with someone who is shy and introverted or a jealous, controlling character with someone who values their independence. Such incompatibilities may have existed beforehand, but were somehow masked, only to become obvious once the relationship was underway. Alternatively, individuals sometimes grow in different directions developing new interests and expectations that draw them apart. As well as mismatches of personality, partners (or friends) often find themselves at odds with one another because their emotional needs are being neglected or undermined.

Whatever the reason, the partners become cut off from one another and energy leaks from the relationship pool. Over time, each of them becomes de-energised and de-motivated as they gain less and less from the relationship. They feel unhappy, uncomfortable and unprotected by the bond itself. As a consequence they begin to withdraw trust, commitment and loyalty. A 'de-coupling' takes place with each partner unpicking the ties that once held them together. They begin to avoid close contact or joint ventures and generally sharing time together, because they fear they will be disappointed and further frustrated. The circuit is never resealed and the energy dynamic is never re-generated because each person is drained of motivation.

The following descriptions of energy-draining games focus on the way they cause partners to retreat from real intimacy while remaining together. These games are typical of several kinds of relationships. First, those at 'the end of their tether', with one or both partners seriously considering a break-up. Second, they are found in relationships in permanent disrepair in which trouble is 'a way of life' for partners. Finally, such energy-draining games may be combined in particular relationships – some having a dominant influence while others are simply side games.

Manipulative games

These games are focused on the constant manipulation of power which monopolises the attention of both partners. The more powerful partner has to be in the driving seat in order to get what they need from the relationship – whether it is love, security, recognition, validation or whatever. Generally, the need to dominate derives from an initial insecurity (perhaps about not being good enough to hold on to a partner). If the weaker partner asserts his or her independence, it is seen as a threat, triggering a fear of abandonment and loss of control over the other. One way of preventing any loss is to unsettle and undermine the other psychologically, perhaps by chipping away at her or his self-esteem, self-confidence or feelings of competence or self-value. This keeps them unsure and hence they remain under the thumb of the more dominant partner who attempts to steal energy from them. The partner is drained of their life-force energy (both physical and emotional) in a subtle, but parasitic fashion. The more passive they are as personalities, the less will they be aware that this is happening. In fact, they may think that their low self-esteem, and unhappiness, is 'natural' – the inevitable trade-off for their dependency.

Of course, the more a partner challenges and resists both will be drawn into an energy-sapping power struggle. But what does a dominant partner get out of the situation? Are they filled with life-affirming energy? Not at all, in fact their behaviour is self-defeating. Whilst their domineering behaviour is designed to gain the security and unconditional acceptance they crave, any sense that they might actually achieve this is fleeting, elusive and ultimately illusory. In the final analysis they are left feeling emotionally flat, the result of a hollow victory. There are two main reasons.

First, although they want to be completely in control they can never take this for granted because his or her partner always retains some residual independence. Thus they are haunted by a continuing sense of insecurity that their precious 'control' may be challenged at any point in the future. Second, after an initial buzz of 'having it their way', the dominant partner begins to feel emotionally short-changed because they sense that the psychological support they gain has been obtained fraudulently. Manipulation (whether blunt and obvious, or more subtle and emotional) may bring a veneer of security, self-confidence and self-esteem, but it cannot bring the real thing. Genuine emotional ful-filment requires the use of benign influence – it cannot be stolen or extracted without the willing and empathic participation of another. It would take a great deal of self-deception for a manipulative person to be totally unaware of this. So, far from being an energy booster for the dominant partner, manipulative games actually deplete energy.

The games, therefore, are symbiotic in which the partners are locked into a mutual dependence, but for different reasons. For manipulation to work properly, the dominant partner needs someone who will accept their control and not put up too much resistance. In turn, the submis-sive partner becomes reliant on the other's influence because it creates structure and organisation for their life. At the same time it allows them to abandon many responsibilities.

Variations on the theme

Manipulative games appear in different forms. Although they always involve the rather bullying intimidation of one partner by another the extent and intensity of this can vary. At one end of the scale the bullying can take the form of emotional manipulation with either no indication or only the merest hint of physical threat to back up control. At the other end of the scale, of course, we have full-blown emotional terror-ism and physical abuse (as in 'domestic abuse' involving both women and men). While this more serious and aggressive form has received most attention in research, the less intense versions are probably more widespread. They are found in those relationships in which one part-ner tends to take the lead and make decisions over important matters through sheer force of personality, psychological manipulation, stub-bornness, criticism, heavy-handed argument, intimidating comments or even implicit threats of physical coercion.

Although the game is a favourite preserve of males, women, too, are just as capable of playing the lead role. But the personalities of the part-ners as well as their gender also play a crucial part in determining who will play the 'lead' or 'submissive' roles. Furthermore, a person who is dominant in one relationship may, in another, be happy to accept a more subordinate position – as I shall now illustrate with reference to John Lennon's two marriages. A different partner and different circum-stances may bring out different emotional needs in the same person and thus reveal a different side to their personality. This, in effect, is what seems to have happened when John Lennon moved from his first wife Cynthia to his second, Yoko Ono.

The marriages of John Lennon

John Lennon's first marriage was to Cynthia Powell and she has written about her life with him in the early years, both before and after the success of the Beatles. Cynthia (Lennon 2005) suggests that before they married, John was a rather insecure suitor. The insecurity can be clearly traced to three critical events in his early life. First, at the age of five he was required to choose between staying with his mother or father when their relationship broke down. Second, having chosen his mother, he subsequently had to endure the heartache of being separated from her (age seven), because living with his aunt was thought to be the more practical option. Third, at the age of fifteen he was severely traumatised by the death of his mother, whom he idolised.

During his adolescence John kept these painful memories, and the psychological insecurities that they generated, well hidden from everyone around him. He adopted a persona that presented a tough, sometimes deliberately cruel, outward appearance to the world, even seemingly enjoying other people's misfortunes. Underneath, however, he remained troubled by his hurtful childhood memories and this softer and extremely vulnerable side was glimpsed by only a few of those close to him. When he met Cynthia at art-college his insecurity manifested itself in periodic jealous rages for what (he imagined) was her showing interest in other men. At one point Cynthia recounts that John hit her because she had danced with a mutual friend – although it was entirely innocent – and this led her to seriously question the incipient relationship.

Whilst not condoning this behaviour, it is fairly easy to conclude that John's jealousy was prompted by his childhood memories (and continuing fears) of abandonment – first by his father and then his mother. In such situations a child will fear abandonment because he or she imagines they are not good enough to retain the love of their parents – in John's case, his mother in particular. The jealous rage is, without doubt, an expression of pain by an already hurt and vulnerable person. But it is also his (or her) attempt to thwart an anticipated loss of their partner – and thus crucially, a loss of control over this person's affections – by nipping it in the bud before it happens. It is a means of seizing control before control slips away. Of course, the anticipated loss is all in the mind of the beholder, but this doesn't make the anxiety any less real.

This kind of behaviour exhibits some of the classic features of manipulative games. The pattern of these initial attempts at control was repeated over and over again in John's subsequent marriage to Cynthia and became a routine feature of their relationship, with John adopting the active dominant role while Cynthia was the passive, submissive partner. As with the incident of violence that Cynthia records – for which she forgave John and took him back – in her marriage as a whole, she exhibited a sequence of similar 'forgiving' (and thus submissive) behaviour based on her belief that beneath his macho exterior there was a tender and vulnerable child that needed to be understood.

Indeed, it seems, what kept her committed to the relationship (although she does not explicitly say this) was the thought that she could rescue his 'vulnerable child' from the clutches of his more aggressive and dominant self (see Chapter 7). In short, her long-term project was to recover his tender loving side that she herself had been privy to only in brief glimpses, in between the more distracted, detached and controlling behaviour he usually adopted with her. However, this project was rudely interrupted once he had met Yoko Ono and embarked on an affair with her. Once this had happened, his relationship with Cynthia became something of a tiresome obstacle to John. She was dispatched, eventually, in a rather cruel and dispassionate manner, being 'thrown out of her own home' without any protest or attempt at resistance. This, of course, simply reinforced the notion that she was a passive object willing to be shunted around at the behest of her husband who, incidentally, even falsely accused *her* of infidelity.

John's subsequent relationship with Yoko was based on entirely different principles to the one with Cynthia. Two simultaneous changes seemed to underpin this radical alteration. First, John's tough, aggressive and frankly egocentric self, which had predominated for so long, had been muted and softened due to the influence of the vast amount of drugs he was using. Combined with this was the fact that his complete absorption in Yoko at this stage revived early feelings about his mother. Indeed, John came to identify Yoko as a mother figure, one in whom he could involve and surrender himself almost entirely (Goldman 1988, Seaman 1991).

As a complement to his newly acquired passivity, and in stark contrast to Cynthia, from the start, Yoko assumed the dominant role in the relationship. She assumed the role of parental figure protectively guiding her charge through the conventional world of networking and business deals that John so despised. Later, in their marriage she assumed entire control over John's financial and business affairs which gave him the freedom to indulge himself in whatever distractions he wished, including, of course, his song writing and recording. But she also 'managed' him emotionally. In this respect he was more dependent on her than she was on him. She even suggested at one point that he should take a lover (an associate of hers called May Pang) because she needed a break from his overwhelming dependence and reliance on her. However, once she decided she was ready to take him back she instructed him to abandon Pang and summoned him back to their New York apartment. By all accounts John meekly submitted to these demands seemingly completely in the thrall of Yoko.

With his almost total emotional and practical submission to Yoko, we have here a complete reversal of the relationship with Cynthia. Instead of John being dominant he is now the passive partner with Yoko being stronger and more pro-active. The cause was threefold. First, there was a change in John's personality; and second, Yoko brought out a different side of his personality – the vulnerable child to her mother parental figure. Finally, as the new partner (Yoko) responded to him quite differently – she wouldn't tolerate his aggressive bullying side and, in fact, taught him how to be submissive and respectful towards women. John moved from a game in which he was the instigator and focal point of the manipulations that characterised his first marriage, to a subsequent game in which he was now the object of his partner's orchestrations.

The more general point illustrated here is that the players are not necessarily permanently stuck in their game roles – although, of course, while they remain in a particular relationship their roles and behaviour may be relatively fixed. However, a change of partners may open up the possibility that dominant and submissive positions in one relationship may be reversed in another.

Games of attrition

These games usually indicate an advanced state of deterioration in a relationship and are associated with 'pretence' intimacy in which the partners put up a nominal show of closeness while in the company of other people, but actually feel little or nothing for each other. The partners may once have been 'closer' but the feeling that one or both partners 'will never get it right' generally marks a rapid reduction in the quality of intimacy. If, indeed it started out as 'dynamic' intimacy it quickly passes through 'episodic' and 'semi-detached' phases, ending up with the unsatisfactory compromise of 'mutual pretence'. In this sense attrition is primarily an endgame rather than an interim one. Unlike manipulation, in games of attrition partners are relatively equally matched although they may approach the game differently – for example, using 'offensive' versus 'defensive' styles of conflict.

There are two main variants of games of attrition although both involve some manipulation. In the first, one person initiates the game and keeps it going while his or her partner uses defensive and/or 'counter-attacking' manoeuvres. The game is rather one-sidedly energy draining. The 'initiator' slowly tries to grind the other down with persistent criticisms and comments designed to undermine their morale, competence and self-confidence. In response a partner may put up a spirited resistance based on counter-attack or self-justification. This may be the pattern over a considerable period of time, but eventually, the unending put downs and criticisms wear them down. He or she becomes 'battle fatigued' and resigned to the fact that the relationship will never provide them with emotional satisfaction.

If the 'lead' or 'initiator' of the game habitually relies on indirect communication then they are more likely to use nagging, whingeing and emotional blackmail to wear down the 'opposition'. In response the other partner may deliberately tune out of the constant barrages and thus remains aloof to them. However, in the process the target may further infuriate the initiator who may step up his or her attack. The target may launch periodic counter-attacks when the initiator's critical jibes finally strike home. On the other hand, being subjected to constant nagging a person may respond in kind by trading critical comments on a one-to-one basis. In this sense the counter-attack is an attempt to reassert 'authority' (that is, 'control') in response to insistent attempts to undermine it. If, however, the 'lead' habitually uses direct communication, the weapons of choice will more likely be comprised of criticisms, complaints, 'interrogation' and 'surveillance'.

An example

To further illustrate how this works and what I mean by 'interrogation', let me draw from my own personal experience – the relationship between my parents (both of whom passed away some time ago). My father was an excellent example of the lead player in a game of attrition with my mother as the counter-attacking partner responding to his never-ending complaints and criticisms. Any aspect of domestic life could become the focus of his negativity and disapproval and my mother was always blamed for whatever it was that bothered him. If his shirt collars were not cleaned perfectly, if he found dust anywhere in the house, if she failed to iron an item of clothing to his exacting standards he would begin – in a low key way at first – to let his objections be known.

But these objections didn't just take the form of isolated comments bluntly expressed and quickly forgotten. They were woven into a ceaseless carping commentary on the unsatisfactory state of affairs – why it had arisen and how it could have been avoided. The sequence would build and build with her fending off the flow of tedious barbs until eventually, she would explode in rage. The next phase would be a full-scale shouting match with her becoming increasingly volatile and aggressive whilst he continued to stoke things up with his endlessly repeated criticisms and comments. The third phase would be mutual withdrawal into a vicious spiky silence punctuated by periodic outbursts – the overflow of after-thoughts on the subject. The subsequent atmosphere would be unbearably tense, with my parents hardly able to tolerate each other's presence. This uneasy cessation of hostilities would last until the next round was initiated by yet another of my father's complaints. And so the pattern would be repeated *ad nauseam*.

However, my father's irritations were not limited simply to what he considered to be his wife's infractions of her domestic 'duties and responsibilities'. He would routinely interrogate her as to what she had said and to whom, where she went, and what she did when she was out of his immediate presence. He was particularly concerned about *exactly* what she said to other people, the minute details of the conversation or gossip that had transpired and which friends, neighbours or (extended) family members were privy to which bits of information. This behaviour was partly caused by his desperation to keep a secret of the fact that he was unemployed most of the time (and couldn't hold down a job anyway, because of his lack of social skills).

Of course, this made him paranoid about controlling information about himself and the economic status of the family. Thus his surveillance and interrogation techniques, as they were practised on my mother (and me to a growing extent), were designed to restrict the flow of information and preserve his 'terrible secret'. But he used these techniques in the same manner as his general complaining and criticism. Instead of a brief, one-off exchange he would keep on and on asking, probing, demanding, double-checking the facts, searching for any perceived weaknesses in your story, making sure you were telling him everything, over and over again, driving my mother (and me) crazy.

Incidentally, as the references to my own involvement may have suggested, children who witness such relationships are not simply external bystanders. They are as much a part of the relationship as the couple themselves and as such they live out the emotions, tensions and conflicts of the partners. In this sense the anxieties and fears that the children 'inherit' from this experience begin to have a life of their own. In my case until I was in my teens I was extremely anxious and fearful that my mother (who was the central block in my emotional stability) might leave him (and thus abandon me) and that I would be left to fend for myself against 'him'.

Other variants and aspects of the game

Instead of just one person leading the 'fault-finding', a variant is when both partners alternately take the lead role in a competitive struggle whereby each tries to wear the other down. Thus in trying to rob one another of energy they drain themselves and the relationship of all momentum and intimacy. Eventually, both partners feel resigned to their mutual incompatibility and to a total compromise of their hopes, wishes and desires. Because they are both 'victims' – or 'losers' – in the game, they are responsible for creating their own emotional prison. Any 'intimacy' they show each other is mutual pretence acted-out simply for public 'show'. In reality, there is little likelihood of any return to a mutually satisfying relationship. In this game of mutual pretence, the partners are likely to adopt a mixture of weaponry and strategies drawn from the repertoires of both direct and indirect communicators.

Both variants of this game raise the crucially important questions of why and how they get started. What causes one or both partners to initiate the fault-finding, game in which the 'other' can never be good enough to satisfy them, can never get it right as far as they are concerned? Two possible scenarios could account for this. The first involves a drastic loss of power and control (of one or both partners) in a relationship that was, at some point, operating fairly normally. Perhaps a serious illness either physical or mental or traumatic event – with an associated loss of self-confidence, self-esteem and competence – may set in train the fault-finding mode.

Alternatively, one or both partners might enter the relationship with a strong sense of powerlessness. An example of this might be those women who are basically limited to the role of housewife, who, faced mainly with domestic chores and menial tasks, consequently, feel trapped and powerless. In this sense, nagging is a kind of protest against their lack of value and influence in the world (Pease and Pease 2002). The example of my father is of an overwhelming sense of impotence born out of two pressures. First, his lack of a job, which meant he couldn't be a 'real' breadwinner, or head of family. Second, his lack of social skills meant that he couldn't influence those around him in the way he would have liked. Both deficiencies thwarted his ambition and culminated in a sense of failure in life – of not being good enough.

Another question concerns the fact that the apparent objective of the lead player is to suck the life-energy from their partner until he or she is broken and defeated. But why would anybody do this? One possibility is that it is a desperate attempt to resuscitate themselves – their self-esteem, competence and power – by simply stealing another's energy. Of course, the game is tragic because it is so comprehensively self-defeating. It drains the energies of each of the individuals and the relationship as a whole to the extent that it creates a huge deficit – a black hole of escaped energy – making any semblance of intimacy impossible.

Emotional withholding games

Although games of emotional withholding are energy draining, in many respects they are less negative and daunting than some of the others. Whereas in the two previous games there is a definite wrecking impulse in one or both partners that pushes towards the destruction of their rela-tionship, emotional withholding is subtler. Instead of breaking down 'the opposition', the individual tries to be as emotionally elusive to a partner as possible thereby softening his or her emotional hold over him or her. The game is one of avoidance, of holding back, of not 'giv-ing' oneself for fear of being revealed as not good enough, or insecure. By remaining elusive it is more difficult to be abandoned in any defini-tive manner. More positively, by being unreachable a person remains in control. Instead of trying to actively control the other, she or he makes themselves uncontrollable.

Often a version of this game occurs in the early stages of relationships, such as in romantic courtship (or 'sussing out' in friendships) where the partners are not giving too much away about their feelings. This has two functions. First, it helps to allay the disappointment of rejection if the relationship doesn't work out for some reason because each person has kept something of themselves and their feelings in reserve. Second, it creates a mystery and a puzzle for the other to work out and which is offered as a 'test' of their feelings and intentions. If the challenge is taken up and the test passed, then the relationship can go forward – it is the signal for the partners to get closer, to trust and commit to one another on a deeper basis. In this sense, games of emotional withholding are played on a provisional basis early on before the relationship is stable.

After this, however, the game is often abandoned as the partners become more and more disclosing towards one another.

However, in some established friendships and romantic partnerships, the game is played on a routine basis and with much greater seriousness and intensity. In these, the game is no longer exploratory. Rather, it has become a means of withholding intimacy or keeping it within certain 'manageable' limits (typical of 'episodic' or 'semi-detached' intimacy). There are three aspects to this. First, the *emotional* withholding or avoidance is only partial. It is not that the 'withholder' is not giving anything at all; rather, they selectively avoid important relationship issues. For example, they may be reluctant to say how much they love and care for their partner, how much they value them, or how much they want to do things together.

Second, at the same time, the withholding or avoidance is a way of keeping control. Avoiding vulnerability seems a crucial part of this game. The player doesn't say 'I'm not available at all'. Rather, he or she communicates to the effect that 'some part of me is available but there is also a secret part of me that isn't', and this is a seductive ploy that keeps the other interested. But this secret part can never be divulged because it would make the person vulnerable and, hence, controllable. Finally, although the withholder keeps control for himself or herself, they simultaneously drain energy from the relationship and, as a consequence, both partners suffer.

Differences in intimacy skills and communication styles

Those individuals who have few intimacy skills may fall into this game unintentionally. Opting for brooding silence or emotional withdrawal may be more the result of an inability to express oneself, than deliberate elusiveness. On the other hand, some indirect communicators may use it as a manipulative ploy. Although not as extreme as emotional bullying or blackmail, it is, nevertheless, extremely effective as a tactic of control. However, most frequently this game is neither unintentional nor deliberate. It seems to be played by individuals who are afraid or insecure about intimacy and disclosure. By holding the other at bay emotionally, he or she tries to be elusive and remain in control, turning an inner weakness into a position of strength in the relationship. It could be argued that someone who is emotionally elusive is almost inviting an emotional rescue response from the other. As noted in Chapter 7 emotional rescuers often convince themselves that they can transform their partners, and thus reveal hitherto hidden, but more acceptable traits or characteristics, only to find that this is a vain quest. Emotional rescuers pursue 'lost causes' in the hope that they can turn things around (De Angelis 1992).

Types of intimate relationship

Games of emotional withholding are linked to three main forms of intimacy. First, where intimacy is deteriorating over time the game marks the move from 'dynamic' to 'episodic' or 'semi-detached' as one or both partners become more and more emotionally distant. Second, in 'episodic' intimacy emotional avoidance may have become the partners' routine way of relating to one another. But if one partner is 'unavailable' while the other wants to be closer, they will become resentful. The tense relationship will be interspersed with periods of uneasy truce and calm in which the problem is neither alluded to, nor spoken about. Third, the game may be played alongside 'manipulative', 'oppressive' or 'pretence' intimacy where there may be an almost permanent state of withdrawal between the partners (Miller 1995, Marshall 2006). In such cases emotional avoidance (or 'unavailability') is used more as an offensive, rather than a defensive, weapon.

In all cases the game may be initiated by one or both,partners. If there is one main initiator, then the game becomes a serial form of emotional hide and seek. A combination of fear and insecurity makes the 'withholder' determined not 'to be pinned down' psychologically and emotionally. Being elusive safeguards against emotional exposure and being accountable to others. Although the initiator is 'in control' it is a negative control by default and this drains energy from the relationship. Of course, there remains the possibility that such a relationship could be revived. However, this requires that the emotional avoider (and/or withholder) gains some insight into his or her 'problem', and is willing and motivated to change. If both partners are emotional avoiders then it is more like a game of chess, with a continuous succession of move followed by countermove in which they drain themselves and the relationship of energy. Neither can see things from the other's viewpoint and the game takes on an aura of a doomed endgame.

Ego-centred games

The two versions of ego-centred games are very much related, but have slightly different emphases. In both games one player seeks attention at the expense of the other. In the first game, 'poor me', the lead player appeals to his or her 'victim' status to grab attention and create pity as well as a 'caring' or 'rescue' response by the other. Such appeals depend on pleas like 'please don't take advantage of me I'm only doing my best'. In the other game, 'look at me', the lead player appeals to his or her inflated sense of 'importance' and status and involves pleas like 'I have so many important responsibilities – they must be given priority'.

In both games the lead player gains attention, sympathy and deference. They drain a great deal of energy because the lead plays mind games with their partner. However, this is not simply to undermine their partner's self-esteem, but rather, because they are totally self-absorbed. In this sense ego-centrism completely dominates both games with the lead consistently grabbing attention from their partner – and thus ensuring that they always come first.

Types of intimacy

These games are mainly associated with 'manipulative' and 'pretence' intimacy. In the first, a person uses their 'victim' or 'important' status while encouraging their partner to be supportive. If a man 'leads', the relationship may gravitate around him because of his 'important' job (and correspondingly inflated ego), while his 'stay-at-home' wife relegates her 'less important' responsibilities. Of course, this mirrors the now somewhat stereotyped division in society between the mainly male 'public domain' of work, business and careers, as compared with the private, female domain of family life, housework and childrearing (Smith 1988, Cameron 2007). In the public domain general intimacy, caring and interpersonal relations are subordinated to, and thus neglected, in favour of the family income, consumption patterns, contact networks and so on.

An individual might employ the 'poor me' variant of the game including all manner of emotional blackmails as a means of retaining attention in the relationship. Thus his or her pleas and appeals may include 'after all the sacrifices I've made', or 'after all I've done for you', or 'all the support I given you', to 'I could handle this if my health wasn't so bad', or even 'I always seem to be the one who gets hurt'. In either case (man or woman as lead) the manipulator tries to guilt trip their partner into accepting that their desires and interests come second in the relationship. But it is important to recognise that in 'poor me' or 'look at me' the partner is not coerced or intimidated. The partners are 'willing slaves', and may even be actively supportive of their spouses or partners. For all intents and purposes, they are 'happy' with the role offered to them and in this sense the union could be described as 'harmoniously imbalanced'.

By contrast, when these games are linked with pretence intimacy, neither partner is willing to accept a subordinate position. Private deals and pacts serve to equalise the apparent differences in power and control. For example, a housewife who enthusiastically supports her husband may do so only if her husband allows her to call the shots in the more private, domestic sphere. Thus, for example, she may have the deciding vote in many important matters concerning intimacy (such as lovemaking, disciplining the children, family relations – who is invited over, who is visited – and so on). In this manner the public image of the couple as one in which a particular partner is thought to 'wear the trousers' may be an illusion – because both wear them in different contexts.

With pretence intimacy, in the 'poor me' and 'look at me' games both partners take the lead – although perhaps at different times. Appealing to either their victim status or their greater 'importance' provides one, or both, with a means of 'stealing' energy from the other. Interestingly, both partners may play the same game, trying to outwit one another at every turn. Thus they might try to 'out-victim' or 'out-rank' one another in an attempt to bag more attention and energy from a rapidly depleting reservoir. In such a case claiming to be a victim is used in a more aggressive fashion as a means of gaining the upper hand in the relationship.

Addictive or co-dependent games

These games revolve around the shared fears, insecurities and dependency needs of the partners. Because of their psychological vulnerabilities they become over-reliant on one another. But the price they must pay for the protection afforded by their bond is some loss of their identities as individuals. Protective unity is achieved at the expense of independence and self-reliance. Clearly, the partners inhabit a self-imposed prison but are also painfully aware that they can't easily escape from it. Thus, both partners secretly harbour feelings of resentment.

Unpredictable as it may seem, intimacy in these games is a mixture of the genuine and phoney. The partners possess two overriding, but strongly opposing needs. Their primary need is to maintain the loyalty, support and commitment of their partner so that they continue to be a source of psychological support and confirmation of themselves as individuals. But this cuts into their ability to give genuine affection, care and love. Every expression of care and tenderness is compromised by the need to enslave the other. Thus seduction is always interlaced with phoney elements. The need to grab and maintain the other's attention at all costs is overriding. Constant mutual surveillance breeds a special kind of paranoia in which each partner checks out where the other is going, what they are doing and with whom. Other people (potential lovers, friends or even intrusive relatives) must not threaten their mutual dependence. Another side effect is an unbearable claustrophobia that produces a reflex need to create personal breathing space. Thus, periodically partners may feel the need to be free from the straightjacket in which they find themselves. But, of course, this is compromised by their equal hunger for the self-confirmation that their partner supplies.

In addictive (or co-dependent) intimacy (Peele and Brodsky 1974, Giddens 1992, Norwood 2004) the individuals are both active manipulators and, at the same time, passive victims of their partner's manipulations. That is, partners are simultaneously both subject and object of game strategies. In other energy-draining games, individuals are required to play only one role at a time. Thus they can either be manipulators or victims, but not both manipulators and victims at the same time. In general, co-dependent games thrive on a duality of outward loyalty and disguised deception. It is in the interests of both partners to shower each other with compliments and 'positive strokes' (Berne 1966) in order to keep one another sweet and to perpetuate an image of unity. Indeed while they outwardly stress 'togetherness', it is, in fact, all about keeping an eye on one another. The relationship looks for 'all the world', as if it was in 'good order' whereas in reality it masks an oppressive mutual over-dependence.

Beneath the apparent unity and harmony, there lies suspicion and mild paranoia. Partners scrutinise one another's most commonplace comments and utterances in case they contain hidden messages. Checking one another's whereabouts and meetings with 'outsiders' becomes the stock in trade of both partners. In some cases, cutting off from former friends, family and colleagues may be insisted upon because they threaten the 'security' of the relationship (Stewart 1998, Horley 2000, Norwood 2004). Unable to live independently, they thus opt for a pathological unity in which each suppresses the other's freedom while at the same time claiming that they love and care deeply for one another. Some individuals are more likely to be assertive, dominant or competitive, creating dependencies, cutting off a partner from friends, or undermining his or her confidence whilst stressing their own self-importance. Others may be more likely to play the victim, or attempt to emotionally rescue a partner.

Games of addiction and co-dependence are rather unusual as compared with the other energy-draining games because both partners are simultaneously playing the roles of manipulator and victim. Both roles are emotionally destructive and deplete the common pool of energy required to sustain a mutually satisfying relationship. The partners are bound together, but pulling in opposite directions. They are not isolated from each other as they are in other energy-draining games because they need to sustain the illusion that they are a couple. But privately they steal one another's energy and remain emotionally decoupled.

Concluding comment

It is possible for different energy-draining games to be played at different points in a relationship, reflecting changes in a partner's moods, attitudes and circumstances. Alternatively, different games may overlap with each other ensuring that energy from many sources is drained unremittingly from the relationship. Of course, when partners choose to play only energy-draining games, their relationship is likely to remain on a downward spiral of unhappiness. To turn things around they would have to try to reverse the flow of negative energy by deliberately introducing energising elements.

9
Energising Games

Partners feel energised if they have some control over one another's feelings and responses. The sense of aliveness that comes from a satisfying relationship makes them feel vibrant and enthusiastic about life. Thus, a sense of control is essential to feelings of competence. Being successful in social life depends on mutual benign control, in which there is an exchange of emotional (psychic) energy. If a relationship is formed around benign control its non-competitive, creative and intuitive nature will make it more energising. However, if exploitation or manipulation is involved, relationships will be energy draining.

In energising games partners cater for one another's personal needs so as to create emotional closeness. By supporting one another's security, self-esteem, sense of self-worth and so on, they boost their intimacy. In energy-draining games, intimacy needs are thwarted or suppressed by a lack of concern about feelings, interests and desires. In everyday life emotional and identity needs are closely connected with feelings of security and self-esteem (Layder 2004b). Someone low on security is often afraid and anxious and has difficulty with intimate relationships (Laing 1969). A person who lacks self-esteem will feel 'inappropriate to life' (Branden 1985) and its challenges and may shy away from intimate contact. Other personal needs such as self-confidence, love, acceptance and approval, self-worth and self-respect, feeling special and understood, also depend on a foundation of security and self-esteem. In energy-draining games partners tend to attack or undermine these needs while in energising games they are supported and enhanced by the use of positive 'strokes' (Berne 1966).

In this chapter I describe five closely linked energising games, which differ in terms of the psycho-emotional needs they target most. Thus, while one game emphasises approval and acceptance, another might concentrate on individuality or emotional understanding, and so on. Each game 'specialises' in particular emotional and psychological needs. In one sense all emotional needs reinforce each other and therefore the most energising relationships are those in which aspects of all five games play a part. However, if only one game is involved then certain essential needs will be overlooked. For example, in games of 'mutual seduction', love and approval may be in plentiful supply, but identity or communication needs may be neglected.

In energy-draining games control can be achieved in two ways. Either one partner imposes his or her will at the expense of the other, or both partners jockey to gain advantage by skilful manoeuvring or unfair means. In both, communication is 'closed' and imperative (Bernstein 1972) involving little or no debate. Because the controlling partner's self-interests have priority, he or she simply demands or instructs the other.

By contrast, in energising games partners encourage one another to arrive at 'fair deal' agreements and compromises. Although there is some jockeying and competition, each partner is willing to accept less and to acknowledge the other's feelings and wishes. The partners discuss things openly, respecting one another's views, and arrive at agreements based on shared understanding. They exchange emotional 'gifts' of 'comments' and 'opinions' rather than information, instructions or demands. Each recognises that their own needs, interests and desires can only be satisfied if they satisfy those of their partner. It's not a matter of giving 'unconditionally' because intimate relationships are based on the hope that 'loving gifts' will be returned in kind. But partners freely decide whether to return favours and don't respond to threats, intimidation or manipulation. Over time 'giving' will tend to equal itself out, but if one person consistently 'gives' more, he or she may come to question the fairness of the arrangement.

Optimal or mutually satisfying intimacy

Over time intimacy will depreciate or deteriorate if there are continual problems arising from personality clashes, lack of communication and so on. In long-term relationships where partners are living together over-familiarity may cause emotional drift. Knowing someone deeply is double-edged. On the one hand, being 'in synch' with someone may keep the bond ticking over smoothly – as reflected in the phrase 'we know one another so well we can finish off each other's sentences'.

But partners may begin to take one another for granted, creating resentments and leading to emotional drift.

Of course, real intimacy can only survive if partners don't take each other for granted. In this sense, optimal intimacy is always in danger of 'going wrong' and, thus, lasting relationships are those that constantly 'correct' themselves before they go awry. Partners spot problems as, or before, they arise and deal with them constructively. Such relationships are more resilient because partners are ever alert to danger and avoid excessive energy loss and emotional drift by continually reviewing and redefining their relationship. It's not that energising games are completely free of disruptive elements. Rather, by approaching problems constructively and reflectively partners avoid getting bogged down. In contrast, partners in energy-draining games are continually stealing energy from each other. They are on a downward spiral and the relationship is constantly losing energy.

Key themes in energising games

The five energising games cover different aspects of 'dynamic' intimacy. Of course, all relationships get into difficulties and at such times the partners are likely to slip into bad habits – particularly selfishness and manipulation. If intimacy is truly dynamic, the partners will quickly return to more benign ways of influencing one another. However, a relationship may hit a period of persistent trouble and intimacy may become 'episodic', or even 'semi-detached', before returning to its initial state (possibly after counselling or therapy). The energising games described here are interlinked but they are distinguishable:

(a) First, energising games differ in terms of how partners (benignly) control and influence one another. For example in games of mutual seduction partners reward one another for positive behaviour. Thus they are encouraged to carry on with energising behaviour while avoiding selfishness, whereas in identity-affirming games control and influence takes place through the medium of ego grooming.

(b) Second, energising games differ in the manner in which they spotlight and 'work on' specific personal (identity and emotional) needs. Thus, mutual seduction emphasises acceptance and approval – essential for a strong and stable sense of identity – whereas altruistic games stress the protection of the bond (Figure 9.1).

Game	Benign control	Need
(1) Mutual seduction games	Reward/reinforcement	Love, acceptance and approval
(2) Identity-affirming games	Ego grooming	Recognition of individuality
(3) Empathy games	Empathy/rapport	Being understood
(4) Altruistic games	Altruism/benevolence	Protection of the bond
(5) Mutually supportive games	Co-operation/mutual respect	Balance of independence and dependence

Figure 9.1   Energising games

Mutual seduction games

In this game partners benignly control and influence one another by offering love and affection. They behave in the spirit of giving (rather than taking) in the sense that each is willing to make the first move. The partners mirror acts of love, kindness and appreciation and emphasise the importance of 'unconditional' love. However, in practice it is usually expected that love will be returned in kind at some future time. Indeed, if one person believes that they are 'giving' too much as compared to their partner then they are likely to withdraw emotionally. Thus while there is *roughly equal* give and take, a relationship will be continually re-energised, but if this becomes imbalanced, energy will drain from it.

Without doubt, love, acceptance and approval are the bedrock of successful intimacy because they help provide security, self-esteem and a robust sense of personal identity. When love and approval are present, partners feel at ease and accept one another's vulnerabilities and shortcomings. The game is reflected in the following comments, which are usually accompanied by hugs, kisses, touches and so on:

'I love you, I appreciate you'
'I want to do this for you'
'I want to give you this as a token of my gratitude'
'You deserve all the love and support I can give'
'I am so lucky to have you'
'I would do anything for you'
'You mean so much to me'
'I don't know what I'd do without you'

'I can always depend on your warmth and enthusiasm'
'You are always there when I need you'
'Give me a hug'
'You'll never change, but I love you still'

Acceptance is not simply an empty expression of tolerance. It means 'I accept you for yourself with all your limitations and imperfections'. Similarly, 'approval' doesn't have to be asked for, or earned. In a loving relationship approval is given almost without thought – 'you don't have to ask for my blessing, you know that you already have it' might be an expression of this. Love, acceptance and approval promote trust and loyalty. They express the sentiment 'you have my trust and I have yours'. Physical or verbal gestures of love communicate the value of one another's company and reflect the basic need for social connectedness, which, in essence, is a way of staving off feelings of loneliness. Clearly, partners benignly influence and control one another's responses in an effort to satisfy their own needs and desires as well as their partner's, but mutual satisfaction also occurs through the seductive power of gifts and persuasion. The seductive effects of persuasion in particular play a crucial part in these games.

The game is complicated by the fact that some research has shown that men and women tend to express love in different ways (Cancian 1987). Some men express love by practical help, financial support and sexual desire whereas some women emphasise talk and the exchange of affection – although, of course, these roles may be reversed in many situations. Clearly, intimate communication is central to mutual seduction and when this game is going well, both partners 'give' on an equal basis. But a person who is naturally 'more giving' may take on more than their fair share of emotional responsibility in the relationship. Such a person may also be ripe for manipulation. In this sense, the game can remain energising only if there is a genuine balance of responsibilities.

Identity-affirming games

In these games partners pay attention to one another's individuality – their unique special qualities – and they benignly influence and control each other through ego grooming. Here 'ego grooming' doesn't refer to inflating a partner's sense of importance by feeding him or her false information – say by flattery, or pretending they are better than they are, or that they are superior to others. Rather, partners 'home in' on one another's special qualities, and frequently show their appreciation through gestures and comments. Deep knowledge of one another's skills, strengths and vulnerabilities enables partners to benignly guide and shape each other's feelings and responses.

Treating one another as 'special' therefore reassures partners that their unique needs and desires will be taken into account. As a result, each becomes more cooperative and eager to please. For example, a person will be more likely to please a partner if he or she feels regarded as special. This 'wanting to please' the other is reinforced if trust and respect are also present and identity-affirming games emphasise these qualities. Respect is also enhanced if one partner knows that the other values their unique qualities, and vice versa. The following are phrases, comments and themes that are typically expressed in this game – again, usually accompanied by appropriate body language – facial expressions, touch, eye contact and so on.

'You are such a thoughtful person'
'I appreciate what you do/did for me'
'Others like the way you make them feel important'
'I know how vulnerable you are'
'You worry about these things don't you?'
'Your inner strength makes you stand out from the crowd'
'You always stick up for others'
'I love you for the kind of person you are'
'You are incomparable/irreplaceable'
'You're the kind of person who gets things going/organised'
'You always raise my spirits/I love your sense of humour'
'You make *me* feel special'
'You always see the best in others'

Appreciation of individuality goes right to the heart of a person's self-identity, their own sense of themselves. Thus, reassurances of uniqueness buttress a person's sense of realness, authenticity and security in the world. They also build self-esteem and a readiness to 'take on' the world (other people). Since both security and self-esteem needs are central in identity-affirming games then they may become an important foundation of an energising relationship. Because the personal identities of the partners are the focal point, they provide a firm anchorage for emotions such as love and approval.

But an appreciation of a partner's individuality also feeds into other elemental feelings and needs. In particular it helps in establishing a person's competence and efficacy in terms of what they can do and what they think they can accomplish. An individual must be able to rely on himself or herself to deal with any life problems that arise. He or she must be confident of making things happen and feels that they are not simply being 'pushed around' by forces beyond their control. Partners who regularly affirm each other's individuality, therefore, support one another's self-confidence. The message sent out is that both partners are strong and reliable and can be 'depended upon'.

Each time a person's unique qualities are noticed and given attention, the importance of their independence is underscored. This is crucial because if a person lacks full independence – that is, if they remain largely dependent on others for approval, for self-esteem and so on, then this will tend to upset the balance of power and control in the relationship. Of course, in one sense the pull towards independence would seem the opposite of companionship, friendship or even romance. But independence and togetherness are equally important human needs. We all need some personal space as well as connectedness with others (Layder 1997, 2004a). However, as individuals, we vary in how much we want of these things and sometimes this makes it difficult to strike the right balance. Honouring one another's special qualities, however, may go some way towards achieving a working balance because it allows – even encourages – partners to be clearer about how much they value their independence (or personal space) as against their need for involvement and connectedness.

In mutually satisfying intimacy there is some merging of the partners' identities, in so far as they tend to see themselves as a couple rather than separate individuals (Perel 2007). But it is equally important that a person's identity is not lost, confused or swamped by the other's influence. Truly energising games require a balance between the independence and the involvement of the partners (Layder 2004a). Being one's own person in terms of what an individual thinks and does, and not simply 'fitting in' with other's wishes must be balanced by a willingness to accommodate partner's needs and interests. If partners attend to other essential relationship requirements, such as making time for one another, then mutual respect and trust will be reaffirmed and gratitude and pleasure will be generated (Reibstein 1997).

In optimally energising intimacy partners respect and value one another's unique identities and personal qualities. Thus identity-affirming games are crucial since everyone needs to be recognised and valued for who they are as individuals – their personal identity. However, there do seem to be differences in terms of which aspects of individuality are most highly valued. Some individuals tend to value independence more than involvement and hence it might *seem* that they would be more at ease with this game while those who value togetherness more might be less so. However, it may simply be that such people favour the 'independence' aspects of personal identity whilst those favouring togetherness focus on identity in terms of the special contribution it makes to an intimate relationship. Clearly, both aspects are important for a balanced sense of identity since each stresses different but complementary aspects of individuality or 'specialness'.

However, from this angle a stress on 'independence' may prevent a person from properly understanding that intimacy is a good source of identity support. In this respect those who over-value independence may become cut-off or estranged from intimate relationships. On the other hand, underrating the importance of 'independence', as a source of individuality, may result from an over-valuation of togetherness. Thus, such individuals may lack this as a potential identity support. Of course, a benefit of valuing involvement and connectedness is the avoidance of social isolation. In general, identity-affirming games require attention to both aspects of identity with partners honouring one another's special individuality while also balancing the demands of independence and togetherness.

Empathy games

These games are not about understanding as in 'understanding' what someone is saying. Understanding, here, indicates knowing what makes a partner 'tick' or what fires their passions, how they jell with others. In this sense, 'understanding' enables partners to benignly influence and control one another through empathy, rapport and emotional attunement (Scheff 1990, Collins 2005). To some extent this overlaps with identity-affirming games because emotional understanding often goes hand in hand with appreciating a partner's special qualities. However, there are crucial differences. In identity-affirming games the primary emphasis is on appreciating and understanding individuals for *who they are*, whereas in empathy games the emphasis is on understanding them on the basis of *how they feel*, on their passions and desires. Understanding a person for 'who she or he is' is based on individuality, whereas being understood in terms of personal feelings is founded on shared experiences and emotions. The latter are reflected in the following comments:

'I understand how you feel'
'You know why I'm sad'
'What concerns you, concerns me'
'We feel the same way about things'
'You always seem to get on well with others'

'I know what's going through your mind'
'We've been through so much together'
'I feel so close to you'
'I can tell when you're in a good mood'
'This kind of thing upsets you'
'We work well together/we seem to click'
'I don't have to ask, I just know how bad you feel'

Such remarks and comments grow out of the shared experiences and emotional bonding that energise intimate relationships. Combined with hugging, putting arms round shoulders, kissing, gazing and so on, such comments convey emotional rapport, support, empathy and attunement. Above all, empathy games depend on *how* things are said rather than *what* is being said (Austin 1962). It's not only the words themselves but also the meta-messages of feeling and empathy that are crucial in conveying that a partner is truly understood. He or she must be convinced that what is said is not simply a string of 'empty' words put together in order to produce an effect – to get him or her 'on side', so to speak. They want to know that what is said is really meant, because *their* emotional life is at stake. In order for them to feel valued, appreciated, loved and cared for, these things must be conveyed authentically and sincerely.

By engaging in empathy games partners are reaffirming their bond through experiences, emotions and feelings of pleasure that togetherness can create. At this elemental level deep empathy, frisson and rapport energise and re-energise intimate relationships. The common ground of shared feeling is important because it is the fundamental bedrock of relationships. In fact, it is because of this that differences in personality, needs and desires can be reconciled or overcome. The protective emotional wraparound of an intimate bond makes it a secure refuge that protects us from loneliness. In this sense, empathy games develop over time as the partners' shared experiences build up and their knowledge of one another continues to deepen. But again, it must be stressed that this is an emotional 'knowing' rather than one solely based on facts and information. The substance of the game, therefore, is deep knowledge based on mutual self-disclosure.

Altruistic games

Whereas mutual seduction is about 'giving' in an emotional sense, empathy games stress the more practical side of giving although not entirely in separation from emotional concerns. Whereas mutual seduction is almost wholly about the emotional side of giving, altruistic games focus on both its emotional and practical aspects. In this regard the game is marked out by help and support for one another. Energy is created through the impulse to 'do good' and work in the best interests of one another. In turn, these provide a foundation for security, safety and refuge – in short, the protection afforded by a close relationship. The game is reflected in the following comments:

> 'Our relationship is the most important thing to me'
> 'I'm always here for you'/'you're always here for me'
> 'I know I can depend on you/you know you can depend on me'
> 'We make a good team'
> 'Together we are stronger'
> 'I felt so vulnerable before we became an item/friends'
> 'You know I'll always defend you' (your honour, reputation, interests)
> 'Without your help I wouldn't have got through this'
> 'I appreciate the way you speak up for/support me'
> 'I'm so thankful for all you do for me'
> 'Please tell me if you need anything'
> 'We can overcome this, if we stick together'

In essence, altruistic games celebrate the benefits of togetherness. When it is played properly, both partners enjoy the protective rewards that flow from it. Cooperating as a unit is easier because problems are encountered from behind the security of an alliance rather than 'fighting them out' on one's own. Pleasure and disappointments are experienced jointly and thus their impact is spread around rather than concentrated in one person. Being in a relationship means that one's life agenda (decisions about where and how one lives, whether or not to have children, the network of friends and family that one associates with) are made jointly rather than individually. The benefits that flow from shared, rather than individual, responsibility highlight the importance of connectedness over individual 'differences'. The game stresses the advantages to be gained from at least partly 'merging' one's individuality with a partner's. As long as this 'fusion' of selves is 'in moderation' it can add to a person's security and self-confidence. If it gets out of hand, it may lead to addictive over-dependence. Another danger, as Perel (2007) has suggested, is that too much merging may blunt sexual desire.

However, given that the main focus of altruistic games is a blend of practical and emotional help – how do they differ from empathy games? In the latter emotions do play a role in creating empathy, rapport and understanding, but they are primarily about 'private' feelings. With altruistic games the emotions are mainly to do with the protective alliance (Reibstein 1997) afforded by the relationship. Thus, for example, comments like 'I felt so vulnerable before we met', or 'I appreciate the way you speak up for me', focus on partner's feelings towards one another – their relationship – rather more than individual, private feelings.

Supporting a partner when they are under work pressure, or when they are being criticised or ridiculed are good examples of how a protective alliance works. By taking a partner's side even when not in agreement or when we think they are being unreasonable, loyalty and commitment are extended. A 'we against others' attitude lets a partner know that the two of you are in this together (Gottman 2006). This reinforces his or her sense of security and the value they place on the bond. In such examples, it is clear that feelings of comfort, pleasure and gratitude stem more from the alliance itself than from the unique qualities of the partners – although, of course, these do play some role. However, one person's strength of feeling about sticking together may be rather too much for someone else. An individual might feel they must protect their personal space and independence, and this might lead them to neglect the other's need for support and connection. A delicate balance is required.

Mutually supportive games

This game brings together elements contained in the other four but it also has features that they do not have. In one sense it's the complete opposite of addictive or co-dependent games which are unremittingly energy draining. In the latter, partners simply 'co-exist' and 'survive' in stultifying mutual dependence, rather than genuinely 'live' together. They fear that contact with others might jeopardise the intensity, exclusivity and security of their bond, so they jealously monitor one another's behaviour. Mutually supportive games reverse these emphases completely. Partners encourage one another to freely pursue outside contacts and interests without fear that this will undermine the relationship. The game encourages a working balance between partners' independence and involvement, rather than a fraught and unhealthy symbiosis. The game is reflected in the following comments:

'Let's not fall into a rut, we should try new things together/separately'
'You should develop your talents in. . . . music/art/selling'

'It's good that we have separate interests even though we are very close'

'I'm really happy that you've achieved what you set out to'

'You never stifle my curiosity and I appreciate that'

'I like the way you encourage me to be independent – even though you support me as well'

'I know you value me as an individual and don't treat me simply as...your dutiful wife/husband/partner'

'We don't try to change one another, and we allow each other freedom and space'

'I'm glad you like my friends, they're very important to me'

'Spending time apart from each other can help us appreciate what we mean to one another'

Such comments or exchanges suggest similarities with identity-affirming games in so far as they stress individuality and encourage one another's self-development. Equally however, games of mutual support emphasise the importance of dependence. The game balances dependence on a partner (for love, security, a sense of connection) as well as independence, in order to satisfy each partner's interests, desires and self-development. An over-emphasis on one or the other can only lead to problems. If partners are too independent then 'protective love' (Reibstein 1997) will be overlooked, or even regarded as strange or pathological.

It is certainly true that protective love plays an important role in successful relationships – especially in maintaining optimal intimacy. However, protective love cannot provide everything necessary for good intimacy. For instance, it cannot replace the importance of the continuing self-development of both partners. Each person must feel 'satisfied' with his or her own position in a relationship (what they are getting out of it, as well as what they are putting into it). Of course, what is meant by 'satisfied' will vary considerably. For example, someone may feel they take more emotional responsibility in a relationship but are happy to do so – perhaps in the knowledge that they benefit in other ways. But only when a person feels they have some say in decisions about relationship issues will they accept certain 'responsibilities' and compromises. If someone feels 'forced' to accept a compromise then he or she will begin to feel taken for granted and, perhaps, begin to detach himself or herself emotionally.

Superficially, there is a similarity between this game and addictive or co-dependent games, with partners seeming to constantly monitor one another's behaviour. However, there is a huge difference in the reasons for this. In the energy-draining games, the partners are forever alert to possible disloyalties or threats to the bond, whereas in this one, partners keep an eye on one another for more positive reasons. Instead of *judging* one another's behaviour, partners simply give each other copious amounts of time and attention. They closely 'attend to' what their partner is doing and saying in order to glean what it might mean for the relationship. In this sense, partners' needs, preferences and feelings are minutely examined and sympathetically supported.

This close attention gives rise to respect and appreciation as well as pleasure and gratitude from sharing one another's company. The partners are continually 'sampling' the emotional temperature of the relationship with a view to giving one another 'positive strokes' (Berne 1966) and helping things 'tick over' smoothly. Such sampling requires the use of emotional intelligence (Goleman 1996), in which partners identify and empathise with one another's feelings and respond to their desires and growth needs (Fromm 1971, Maslow 1999). Of course, it is important that these kinds of caring gestures are a constant feature of close relationships, because they reduce the likelihood of taking one another for granted and the resentments this may cause.

Mutually supportive games are not without potential pitfalls. Sometimes an individual's personal development may result in a growing apart of the partner's interests and life goals. This can be made worse when such personal changes upset the balance of power and control in a relationship. For example, if one partner becomes more successful at work, their increased popularity or social status may cause jealousies and resentments. For the game to remain energised these problems must be dealt with constructively. Allowing time and space for one another's personal growth and self-development may help ensure against such problems, but in the final analysis there is simply no way of knowing how personal growth and self-development will work out.

Interweaving games

In a significant sense these five energising games can be understood as different aspects of 'dynamic' or 'optimal' intimacy. Thus a mutually satisfying relationship is one in which all aspects of all the energising games play an equal and substantial role. If all partners' needs are routinely catered for, then the quality of their intimacy will be of the highest order. This doesn't mean that such relationships will always run smoothly. Inevitably, partners have bad moods or display insensitivities, leading to disagreement or hurt which may be destructive of intimacy. Milder forms of emotional bullying, manipulation or blackmail may briefly come to the fore, as tempers flare in the white heat of the moment. However, a characteristic feature of a mutually satisfying relationship is that 'selfish' or 'bullying' elements disappear as quickly as they arrive. Partners deal constructively with such flash points regarding them as atypical and unwelcome intrusions. They are quick to recognise their own mistakes and make-up – thus not letting unresolved conflicts fester into resentments (as 'old scores' to be settled in future disputes).

Games of mutual seduction focus on partner's needs for love, approval and acceptance and underpin their personal feelings of safety and security within the relationship. Identity-affirming games mark out a partner's unique 'special' features thus acknowledging and respecting his or her individuality. Empathy games complement these emphases by focusing on the emotional aspects of individuality – making a partner feel understood in an emotional sense. Altruistic games tap into the elemental need to feel connected, to be part of a 'team' and, in this sense, protect against isolation or loneliness. Mutually supportive games encourage partners to develop individually, but balance this with the 'togetherness' of intimacy. It is essential that the five games complement and reinforce each other so as to produce optimal intimacy.

Relationship rules

Intimacy games must be supplemented by more general 'relationship rules' in order to create genuinely satisfying intimacy. The first is that of simple courtesy. Somewhat paradoxically, it often seems that the closer people are, the more this rule is flouted or forgotten about. But thanking, complimenting or supporting each other on a routine day-to-day basis are crucial for maintaining respect. Unfortunately, intimacy is often regarded as a reason to neglect small pleasantries, expressions of thanks and acts of thoughtfulness. It is as if knowing each other so well makes them unnecessary. But this is a first step towards taking each other for granted – the ultimate enemy of good intimacy. But failing to say thank you for a small favour like a meal or a cup of tea, or cleaning the dishes, can lead to an erosion of respect and a build up of resentment (Reibstein 1997). To keep a relationship alive, being pleasant, tactful, civil, polite and kind is crucial. The standards by which partners are treated must be the same as those normally applied to strangers or work colleagues (Templar 2006).

A second relationship rule emphasises the importance of keeping in touch with each other through talk – the 'keep talking rule'. First and most obviously, talking is an important way of keeping a relationship 'going', of keeping it fresh and alive, whereas habitual silence or non-communication leads to difficulties in relationships. When problems are not shared or talked through, they become amplified (Templar 2006: 128). Not sharing feelings through talk limits the points of connection between partners and inhibits the exploration of new ways of relating. Of course, sometimes silence is appropriate, especially when it signals a kind of sharing that doesn't require words. But silence can indicate lack of interest or excitement in one's partner or the relationship. Without doubt, sharing feelings and experiences is more important for sustaining good intimacy than talking about gas bills or whose turn it is to walk the dog. Talking simply to fill up 'awkward' silences will not do either. Talk must be purposive to keep a bond vibrant.

Being courteous and enquiring about other's feelings exemplify a third essential relationship rule, that of 'making an effort'. The willingness to 'make an effort' adds to the passion, enthusiasm and strength of an intimate bond (Templar 2006: 124). Without this drive to do a bit extra for the sake of the relationship, there will inevitably be a tendency to fall into the trap of taking one another for granted – and is the mortal enemy of good intimacy.

Finally, the rule of respecting privacy is essential for a successful relationship because partners have to be strong together and strong apart (Templar 2006: 114). Allowing a partner their freedom and independence entails respecting their dignity and privacy and, in turn, enhances trust in a relationship.

Energising rules, energising games

General relationship rules play an important role in energising games. All five games complement and reinforce one another by focusing on different emotional and identity needs. As long as these five continue to play important roles intimacy will be optimal. All five games cannot be played with equal emphasis and intensity all the time, but overall there must be some (roughly balanced) attention to each of them. Nevertheless, there will be an uneven emphasis on particular games during the lifetime of a relationship. In a sense each game is a separate stream which, when combined with the others, creates an embracing, energising 'river' binding partners together. Each game contributes to the collective reservoir of energy that underpins mutually satisfying intimacy. But if one (or several) of the games is absent, then the collective strength and flow of energy will be weakened and the relationship will hit trouble. When its tributary streams of energy dry up and peter out, so the overall energy levels fall. The relationship becomes de-energised, and intimacy deteriorates – as when 'dynamic' intimacy becomes 'episodic' or 'semi-detached'.

10
The Erosion of Intimacy

All intimate relationships have their troubles and testing times. None are immune from periods in which partners feel that they aren't getting what they hoped for from the arrangement. Usually, these are 'normal' crises from which the partners recover quickly and resume 'business as usual'. Even the very best of intimate relationships encounters such routine 'turbulence'. However, other problems may be more traumatic and severely test the resolve of the partners. How are these problems created and what consequences do they have? This chapter traces how the unravelling or disappearance of energising games can lead to the downgrading of a relationship – in particular from 'dynamic' to 'episodic' and 'semi-detached' intimacy.

That sinking feeling

In the last two chapters it was suggested that dynamic intimacy is the outcome of five energising games working together in a loose, but coherent manner. So in a sense describing how energising games operate together is also a way of understanding the processes involved in dynamic intimacy. It is probably true to say that many intimate relationships begin life like this with the partners intending and hoping to keep it that way. Unfortunately, for a host of reasons it is also highly probable that sooner or later a great many such relationships fail in this respect. Interestingly, the vast majority of these relationships aren't completely destroyed, but rather, they slowly but surely deteriorate, becoming emotionally flat and de-energised.

Sometimes both partners are aware of the miserable state they have fallen into and are unhappy and dissatisfied. Just as often, they have little idea why it has come to this, or what they can do to get the relationship back on track. Frequently, even though both may be aware that something is drastically wrong, problems and issues remain unacknowledged. Resentments, frustrations and dissatisfactions build up and stay unresolved with both partners living in a sort of quiet desperation. They are resigned to remaining stuck in the relationship either because they can see no alternative or because they are unwilling or unable to do anything about their predicament.

But it may be that one person is prepared to accept things that their partner finds difficult to live with – such as not talking about feelings, or refusing to tackle recurrent problems or 'sensitive' issues. Whether the relationship continues to 'plod along', rather than implode, depends on whether the dissatisfied partner is willing to live with the compromises that accompany the status quo, and/or whether they can summon up the courage to break free. Quite often a partner who is dissatisfied cannot see a way through, and remains in a state of inertia. Nevertheless, despite different levels of tolerance, both partners are trapped in an impoverished relationship.

Sometimes the inertia that keeps a relationship together stems from anxiety and fear of being on one's own. Thus any tie, no matter how unsatisfactory, is thought to be better than none at all. Also, individuals may lack confidence about attracting another partner – and so are prepared to tolerate their plight. Staying with an unsatisfying but known present is preferable to facing an unknown future in which anything might happen. The upheaval and uncertainty associated with breaking away may be overwhelming, especially for longstanding relationships. Partners may feel too old to start over, or have binding financial commitments, or children that make it difficult to make a clean break. Whether or not dissatisfactions are equally shared, and whatever the reasons for them, it is doubtless true that such relationships are no longer mutually satisfying. While not imploding completely, many are badly damaged and consequently slide into 'episodic' or 'semi-detached' intimacy. The next section describes what is involved in this gradual unravelling of energising games.

Which focus: Person or relationship?

In Figure 10.1 above each of the energising games is lined up against its main theme and focus. A useful starting point for examining eroding intimacy is to distinguish between energising games that attend more to the way the partners treat each other as individuals, as compared with those that focus on the nature of their bond. This distinction is more a

Game	Theme	Focus
(1) Mutual seduction games	Love, approval and acceptance	Bond
(2) Identity-affirming games	Individuality	Person
(3) Empathy games	Emotional understanding	Person
(4) Altruistic games	Protection of the bond	Bond
(5) Mutually supportive games	Balance of independence and dependence	Person and Bond

Figure 10.1 Game focus and theme

matter of emphasis than a clear distinction because both elements are involved in all the games.

Games of mutual seduction tend to emphasise the bond because they focus on partners' concerns with social attachment. That is, on how partners' needs for approval and acceptance motivate them to join together as a team, despite any obvious differences in personality, tastes, opinions. In other words, such games centre mainly on things affecting commitment to the relationship. By contrast, identity-affirming games emphasise partner's individual characteristics – those special facets of their personal identities that are the basis of their attraction for each other. They focus on the extent to which they respect (or resent) each other's personal qualities rather than joint or team qualities.

In these respects empathy games are similar to identity-affirming games. They centre on partners' appreciation of each other's unique individuality. On the other hand, altruistic games have more in common with mutual seduction in that primary attention is on the strength of the bond and the practical and emotional protection it provides. Games of mutual support, however, stand alone, since their focus is shared equally between individuality and teamwork. Thus while they support self-development, at the same time, they also stress mutual dependence.

Unravelling games, undoing intimacy

The significance of these emphases is clearer when we examine more closely the move from dynamic to episodic or semi-detached intimacy (bearing in mind, a relationship may deteriorate further into pretence, or manipulated intimacy). If eroding intimacy involves the unravelling of the energising games that make it up, then episodic and semi-detached intimacy represent way stations in this process. For example, in episodic intimacy those games emphasising personal factors rather than the bond (games 2, 3 and 5) are unravelling and disappearing from partners' everyday routines, whilst in semi-detached intimacy they have all but vanished altogether.

The changes are triggered because the personal connection between the partners becomes strained when intimacy erodes. They become more reserved and guarded in their emotional responses. Respect, trust, loyalty and mutual understanding are undermined and disillusionment sets in. Either one or both partners feel the other is no longer the person to whom they were once attracted. Appreciating, having special feelings for, and thinking of the other as 'special' virtually disappear. While games 2, 3 and 5 unravel as dynamic intimacy gives way to episodic or semi-detached forms, games 1 and 4 (focusing on the bond) 'come undone' in a very different manner. They continue to play a role in the relationship although their nature alters considerably.

Let us examine these changes. In dynamic intimacy mutual seduction is about general acceptance and caring although the game focuses on the need for the bond itself rather than on the special feelings partners have for each other. Of course, this is a matter of emphasis, but at this point in eroding intimacy the maintenance of the bond is more important than their love and respect for each other as individuals. Much the same is true for altruistic games, which allow partners to fit together as team members rather than as 'independent' individuals. In this sense, helping one another and being kind and supportive are primarily about investing loyalty and trust in the relationship. Such attitudes and responses reaffirm the protective benefits derived from being in a couple or team.

However, when intimacy is 'on the slide', these games (1 and 4) also undergo subtle changes in character. First, the emotional significance of the games is hollowed out. Partners begin to either drift away from each other unknowingly, or deliberately withdraw psychological investment in the bond. Instead of expressing genuine affection, care, support, loyalty and so on, these games convey the message that 'our relationship remains strong'. In fact, the relationship is increasingly strained as real feelings are replaced by artificial 'public' displays of affection.

Pseudo-affection steadily takes over the personal and emotional content of these games while the bond continues to be important for both partners, even in the face of depreciating intimacy. Paradoxically, because neither partner yet wants to break completely from the relationship, the changes in emotional tenor of games 1 and 4 are accompanied by the increasing significance of the protective benefits of the bond. Until the relationship hits rock bottom it is common for both partners to want to retain some team benefits such as companionship, financial assistance and practical help. Such 'benefits' may even stretch to using the relationship as a safe harbour for exploring emotional or sexual affairs. One or both partners may settle for a less than satisfactory relationship because of low confidence or self-esteem, lack of options, fear of change, financial or emotional commitments (say to children), or even perhaps, in some cases, because of pity for one's partner.

Of course, as long as both partners remain convinced of the benefits of staying together then this will form an outer limit to the erosion of intimacy. But the tipping point will arrive if the process continues unchecked. For example, if tension and conflict reach a point where partners find it impossible to communicate productively with each other then minimal protection or emotional comfort no longer serves as an excuse for staying together. The partners may become 'trapped' in the relationship with no emotional or empathic connection between them. Semi-detached intimacy may sink further down into pure pretence. This process can be further clarified by restating some of the main features of episodic and semi-detached intimacy. These are summarised below.

Episodic intimacy

(1) Intimacy is intermittent and less intense.
(2) Emotional energy and commitment are partly withdrawn.
(3) Relationship is based on compromises and routines.
(4) Intimacy used selectively to manage problems of emotional drift and estrangement (e.g. sex as substitute for emotional disclosure).
(5) Disclosure is less authentic:

   (a) Partners 'engage at a distance' with minimal trust and sincerity.
   (b) Partners selectively withhold their feelings.

(6) Original partner is no longer the sole anchor of trust or sole source of emotional satisfaction.
(7) Restrained intimacy allows more personal space and independence.

Semi-detached intimacy

(1) Frustrated desire for greater closeness.
(2) Concealed anger and unspoken resentments.
(3) Emotional withdrawal and drift because of concealed anger and unspoken resentments.
(4) Relationship of convenience, produced by inertia and/or lack of alternatives.

(5) Disclosure is rare or entirely absent. Partners going through the motions without the emotional rewards. Minimal emotional commitment.
(6) Relationship still offers some 'protection' although constantly threatened by emotional and sexual infidelity.
(7) Partner's focus of attention shifts away from relationship. Trust and sincerity, at a bare minimum. Deception, insincerity and mistrust grow in importance.

Personal control and emotional blocking

Changes in interpersonal control play a huge part in the unravelling of energising games and the emotional blocking that usually accompanies this process. This section outlines the main reasons for emotional blocking, and the cycles of misunderstanding and emotional drift that entrap partners, causing relationships to self-destruct. The cycle may begin as a response to a relationship problem such as a clash of communication styles, disagreements (over practical or emotional issues), personality incompatibilities and so on. Over time, misunderstandings, clashes and arguments grow into long chains of muddled and confusing exchanges between partners, leading them to disvalue (even 'reject') each other's points of view. By not fully appreciating what each is trying to do or say, both partners may begin to filter out (not listen to, or hear) what the other is actually saying. This may concern not only incidental chitchat but also crucial emotional issues such as the expression of intimacy needs. Instead of *talking to* each other, partners tend to *talk past* one another, ignoring important intimacy pleas and deeply felt wishes and desires.

In a similar manner, if partners' intimacy needs conflict this can lead to tension, conflict and misunderstandings about what they want or are prepared to accept. For example, one partner's (excessive) dependency or approval needs may lead the other to cut off, or withdraw. But this may simply create greater 'neediness' and result in further misunderstanding. Clashes caused by different sources of conflict often combine, increasing their impact on relationship troubles. They may kick-start a process in which confusing messages lead partners to hold back emotionally because they are unsure of the other's intentions and behaviour. Uncertainty reduces their confidence about 'making a difference' and with it they lose some of the intensity of their connection with one another. Once this happens the scene is set for further emotional withdrawal.

Actual, or 'felt', loss of personal control and influence turns tenta-
tive withdrawal into fully-fledged emotional blockage. Positive feelings
are slowly but surely replaced by negative, energy-draining behaviour.
Frustration, irritation and anger at being unable to influence a partner's
behaviour may quickly lead to bickering, disillusionment and disappointment. Communication blockage simply reinforces these trends
because the chain of unresolved disagreements and arguments are piled
on top of each other. Partners feel disengaged and their misunderstandings and differences become entrenched.

Feelings of control loss begin as soon as the first cycle of events ends.
With each cycle the partners become more embittered, inhibited and
helpless. They find they can't make the effort to turn things around, and
are thoroughly de-energised. Their emotional drifting apart means that
they are well on the way to complete estrangement seemingly with no
way back. Each cycle of events simply reinforces the effects of previous
ones and intimacy is set on an ever-downward course. This is exactly
what happens when a relationship shifts from dynamic into episodic
and semi-detached intimacy. The loss of interpersonal control experienced by one or both partners opens the door to the negative energy
created by more manipulative and self-serving strategies.

Learning not to talk to one another

A closer examination of this cycle reveals that emotional 'blocking',
communication breakdown and declining mutual influence are linked
to the development of 'bad' relationship habits. One of the most common and destructive of these is the habit of not talking to each other.
The process often happens in a subtle and gradual manner over lengthy
periods of time. Partners may (and usually do) start off from a position
in which they talk fairly regularly about their relationship, their hopes,
wishes and fears and so on. They may not be good at revealing their feelings, and their exchanges may not be the most intense or meaningful,
but they *do* talk, thus keeping lines of communication open.

However, somewhere down the line the ability to connect with one
another breaks down and there is a gradual retreat from talk (particularly about feelings) as a way of being close. This typically happens even
where intimacy remains strong, as partners habituate to each other over
time (Perel 2007). Each feels able to predict what the other is thinking
and what they will say even before they actually do so. In this sense each
feels there is less need to talk since each knows each other so well and
that there is no point in constantly going over the same ground. But

this is a bad idea even in the best of relationships. Partners must remain 'in touch' both superficially, as well as in a deeper sense, to check out the validity of their assumptions about each other. A relationship will die unless it is 'worked at' through the regular exchange and updating of feelings and opinions through talk.

If this kind of habituation (getting to know each other 'too well') is coupled with misunderstandings, clashes of styles or mismatching intimacy needs, then there is even less incentive for partners to talk. The same arguments and disputes will tend to be repeated over and over again, each time with little in the way of resolution or greater understanding. This makes individuals all too aware of their powerlessness – their inability to make a difference to their partner's views or behaviour. Over countless instances of such deadlock, they come to regard talk (and communication in general) as a pointless exercise. Of course, such a vacuum is likely to produce a festering wound, because important things are being left unsaid. Crucial feelings are not expressed, and in their wake leave a trail of misassumptions and ill feelings that remorselessly accumulate over time. But partners caught up in chains of hurtful misunderstanding are also entangled in the cycle of events described earlier. Their lack of influence on each other simply reinforces their hurt, frustration and resentments.

Another reason why the 'keep talking' rule often disappears from a relationship agenda is that certain topics – especially emotional or sexual ones – become taboo, giving rise to mutual inhibition. This may happen if one partner is already sensitive, fearful or inhibited about expressing feelings, or directly talking about intimacy. If a person routinely tries to talk about them, but is met with reluctance or steadfast refusal, an imbalance is created in the relationship. Over time the more enthusiastic partner may also become 'sympathetically' inhibited as he or she realises that their partner is chronically anxious or shy about talking about intimate topics. After a number of failed attempts at discussion, talk in general may be abandoned eventually because of the embarrassment it causes all round. Again, feelings of powerlessness create further emotional and communication blockage.

In addition, once off the agenda a sensitive issue becomes even more highly charged, precisely because it may not be broached. Its very 'unapproachable' nature makes it seem more important. As a result specific problems are intensified because they are left un-addressed and unresolved. The emotional and communication blockage prevents the regular injection of positive energy and positive emotions necessary for closeness. The build up of frustration, irritation and anger, hopelessness, failure and disillusionment can only lead to the more or less permanent estrangement of the partners.

Displaced arguments

When intimacy is under threat emotional blocking may actually cause arguments and conflict. Partners may be sidetracked by seemingly unrelated problems instead of tackling the real ones. In this sense the 'topic' of the argument may have nothing to do with the underlying causes. But when intimacy erodes arguments are usually about thwarted desire and/or the consequences of emotional blocking. Bickering, arguing and sniping often become an accepted way of relating to each other, while problems remain unresolved in the war of attrition.

Conflict styles and eroding intimacy

When intimacy is on the slide, certain conflict styles can only make things worse. For example, in the 'high-level attack' (Quilliam 2001, see Chapter 6) a person explosively vents their anger at the other in a critical tirade. Because this is an off-loading of venom rather than a true exchange of feelings, it offers little chance of any meaningful dialogue. In this sense high-level attacks perpetuate a war of words that has little to do with real relationship problems. Similarly, in the 'retreat' style a person simply removes himself or herself from a conflict situation and refuses to engage in discussion or dialogue. In effect, 'retreaters' deny their own feelings as well their partner's and only worsen any emotional and communication blockage. Both 'high-level attacks' and 'retreat' are particularly destructive of energising games that target individuality, and emotional understanding (games 2 and 3).

'Appeasement' in which a partner backs off from disagreement and denies her or his own feelings is also rather negative in this respect. But because it does not involve an attack on partners' integrity it may work to shore up, rather than undermine, a relationship. Instead, appeasement may allow individuals to enjoy the protective benefits of the bond, even though they may be emotionally withdrawn. However, if used too frequently, appeasement may lead to hopelessness, despair and depression. This is because the suppression of agency and self-efficacy on which appeasement is based is closely linked to the cycle of emotional blocking. Low-level attacks, such as nagging, complaining, being contemptuous and emotional blackmail, similarly, don't involve empathy or connection. They solely reflect the perpetrator's interests and demands and are a constant threat to emotional understanding (game 3) and self-identity (game 2). Usually low-level attackers feel powerless or fearful that they might lose what little they have. The attacks are a rather ineffectual attempt to claw back *a sense* of control by blaming a partner for the failings of the relationship.

High- and low-level attacks, appeasement and retreat (often found in episodic or semi-detached intimacy) may either fuel the cycle of control loss and emotional blocking or be adopted *in response* to particular events or phases in the cycle. These conflict styles contrast sharply with 'win-win' arguments in that they inhibit the exchange of feelings, views and ideas. In some instances there are no arguments at all because partners back away from intense feelings.

Unravelling intimacy and game strategies

In mutually satisfying intimacy partners often refer to themselves as a 'unit' or 'couple' rather than as individuals (games 1 and 4). This serves several purposes. It publicly announces the importance placed on their 'relationship' and implies that others should treat them accordingly. Perhaps more significantly, it is a reminder to themselves that they *are* a unit, bond or team, and not independent individuals. It is also a practical demonstration of their union, closeness and involvement. Such declarations of togetherness pump energy into those games (1 and 4) that support the bond.

Of course, closeness and unity vary over time. When intimacy is visibly declining or under threat, it is no accident that presumptions of unity are regularly contested or questioned. For example, if one person simply assumes their partner will fall into line with their wishes, say by accepting a dinner invitation on their behalf, or suggesting that they are agreed on some issue – without bothering to check, the other may respond by saying 'well you may want to do such and such, but I don't', or 'you may think that, but I have a different opinion'. Hasty reassertions of independence will follow if partners are uncomfortable about being limited to, or eclipsed by, their partner's agenda.

Clearly, as intimacy declines, so does personal and emotional commitment. Increasingly, partners get what they want from each other by using emotionally neutral strategies like clear-cut trade-offs and bargains. Trade-offs and bargains require less full-on sincerity and trust, and thus fit well with episodic and semi-detached intimacy. Nevertheless, some 'phoney seduction' finds a role where there is emotional drift – such as using sex to buy favours, or forgiveness – since it also entails 'soft' manipulation.

Satisfying intimacy thrives on the continual renewal of emotional commitments, obligations and responsibilities. Many relationships fall apart because partners are either not aware of this, or just not prepared to invest the time and effort required. When intimacy erodes and games unravel, partners back away from emotion work because they are unsure about its significance and uncertain about whether they can make a difference. But backing away wrecks the fragile emotional balance of dynamic intimacy. Because of its delicacy, such intimacy can all too easily be destroyed in the rough and tumble of everyday existence.

The problem of habituation

Perhaps the biggest problems for intimacy stem from habituation – getting to know one another deeply, perhaps too well, over time. This is inevitable in any longstanding relationship, but if it isn't carefully handled, it can be the ruin of close relationships. In many cases the effects of habituation are made worse by differences or changes in partner's intimacy needs. One of the trickiest problems is finding the right balance between independence and involvement (Miller 1995, Layder 1997, Perel 2007). This raises very sensitive emotional issues that require subtle handling at the best of times – if, indeed, partners are willing to confront them in the first place. For example, a partner might demand more space and time to himself or herself at various points, while their 'needier' partner may resist such 'pressure'. Tensions around this dilemma can escalate causing great harm to both partners.

Perhaps most damage is done by the growing over-familiarity of partners who come to know one another so thoroughly that they no longer hold the same fascination or interest. If partners are aware of the danger of taking each other for granted, they may make a concerted effort to counter its effects. For example, they might show greater appreciation of the trust and dependability that come from familiarity. In fact, these may provide comfort and stability for the relationship – giving rise to such sentiments as 'I love him (or her) because I know him (or her) so well', 'I know where I am with them', 'I don't have to guess what they want or need, I already know'.

The down side of knowing a partner too well is boredom and predictability, because he or she never does anything that is surprising or exciting (Perel 2007). Partners may have traits and habits that are irritating, and in this sense, familiarity literally breeds contempt. As a result, in some longstanding relationships, partners feel the need to spend more time apart, pursuing different interests and agendas. They begin to drift apart creating more personal space and freedom. This is often the case with episodic or semi-detached intimacy when partners decide to follow different paths while remaining 'together'. Sometimes, however, partners drift apart in an emotional sense because there is nothing to hold them together. They don't particularly want this and don't really know why it has happened, but they feel helpless and powerless to stop it.

Both 'natural' and 'unwanted drift' clearly illustrate the changes in games 1 and 4. The team aspects of a relationship are emotionally neutralised when dynamic intimacy fades into episodic and semi-detached forms. However, neither partner entirely gives up on the relationship itself since it still gives some protection. And although in semi-detached intimacy respect for individuality disappears almost completely, elements of games 1 and 4 remain in vestigial form and keep the relationship together in a purely practical way.

Once a relationship has survived the initial period of getting to know each other and has 'bedded-in', so to speak, the dangers of taking each other for granted are even greater. If partners feel they have exhausted the exploration of one another's personalities, capabilities and potentials, they may begin to assume that there is nothing 'new' to find out. This assumption strikes directly at the heart of one of the most important of intimacy needs to feel special and understood.

Marriage and children

The problems posed by habituation are ever present (and become more important the longer a relationship survives), thus it could be said to be the 'master' problem for intimacy. That is, because it influences and envelops other more particular problems, it also conditions them. For example, the issue of frustrated intimacy needs can be made worse by habituation, as can problems around marriage and children. Emotional drift may be exacerbated by the stresses and strains that attend childrearing. Different strains and tensions may overlay one another, making the overall problem all the more difficult.

With the addition of children, marriage (or cohabitation) this can prove testing for intimacy. Couples sometimes have difficulties with loyalty issues in moving from their birth families to marital or cohabitation partnerships. Questions about whose needs – parents or partners – should be given priority become problematic (Reibstein 1997). Is it feasible or fair to spend more time with parents (say, looking after them if they are ill), than caring for your partner when they are most vulnerable (say, after starting a new job in a new town)?

Reibstein (1997) suggests that the question of divided loyalties is most pressing at the beginning of marriage or cohabitation, because individuals are, perhaps, still uncertain about how much their partner wants and needs them. But there seems no good reason why the problems around divided loyalty should be pertinent only to the early part of a relationship. Such issues can roll on from year to year and never be satisfactorily resolved. In relationships that oscillate between episodic and semi-detached intimacy, partners are sensitive about the authenticity and stability of their 'loyalties' to each other. In these cases, recurrent charges that 'you think more about your parents than me' or 'everyone else comes before me' may become part of an established repertoire of harboured grudges that surface in bouts of bickering and sniping.

For men, a particular problem arises as a result of feeling displaced by the arrival of a child, who claims the attention and affections of their mother, and moves the focus for intimacy away from husbands/ partners. Some men feel pushed to the margins of family life. As Reibstein (1997: 155) notes, 'the frequency and satisfaction with sex declines sharply in the early years of having children ... with the concomitant decline in intimacy'. Couples, especially men, often feel pushed apart by this. Men may develop more distant emotional relationships with their wives/partners. Of course, this can breed dissatisfactions and strains in relationships, which, before children, were close.

The middle years of parenthood, when children become more independent and begin to leave, is another sensitive period for partners. They now have more time to spend with each other, but if they do not use the increased time to refocus on each other – to 'get to know' one another again – it sends out a message that they have a low priority for one another. Even if this is not actually said or implied, it is a tacit 'void' in the relationship that has massive emotional resonance. It is a time when partners may realise that they don't have (or no longer have) as much in common as they thought.

Their disappointment and lack of connection in these years may lead to emotional and communication blockages. More seriously, but typical of semi-detached intimacy, partners may begin to search for satisfaction outside the bond. So in the post-children phase of a relationship emotional estrangement may increase as partners find that they want to spend less and less time together. They may become disillusioned with the 'quality' of the relationship and disappointed that they won't be spending their later years looking after, and caring for each other.

Turning points and crises

Clearly, partners have little control over unforeseen critical incidents such as illnesses, deaths, losing jobs, bankruptcies, disabling accidents. Such incidents can severely test a relationship at the best of times, but they can be particularly damaging when coupled with eroding intimacy. Other turning points and crises may arise from clashing styles or mismatching personalities or intimacy needs. Of course, partners may not be aware of these problems at the start of a relationship so their destructive effects may take a while to make themselves felt. They may develop into crises, which either cause an 'upward spiral' (Reibstein 1997) towards reconciliation and closeness, or down towards further erosion.

Frequently crises emerge because a partner's personal development precipitates a split in interests, friends, goals and plans. Typically, partners change over time or simply fall out of love (the influence of habituation). Although there may be no bad feelings, difficult decisions may have to be made about whether to stay together. But changes may also occur as the result of conscious attempts at self-development. For example, upgrading educational or occupational skills may prise partners apart. Such personal growth may boost a person's power and self-confidence, but may also alter the balance of power in a relationship making it difficult for partners to adjust.

Whither intimacy?

Eroding intimacy is not necessarily a one-way street – sometimes it heralds the resuscitation of a faltering relationship. However, in many cases partners 'fall out of love', 'lead lives of quiet desperation', or 'are trapped in an unhappy marriage'. Such eventualities are reflected in remarks and comments such as 'I've lost respect (trust) for' or 'loyalty to him or her', 'I'm being taken for granted', 'we are drifting apart' and so on. Such comments indicate a slide from dynamic through episodic, to semi-detached intimacy – sometimes even further into the pretence, oppressive or manipulative types.

11
The Nature of Modern Intimacy

At this point it is appropriate to return to the issue of the nature of modern intimacy by comparing the account developed in Chapters 2–10 with that of the 'pure relationship' (Giddens 1992, Beck and Beck-Gernsheim 1995). On the basis of evidence presented in Chapter 2 modern couple intimacy is not uniform and unitary and thus the pure relationship overlooks its finer gradations and complexities. The typology of couple intimacy in Chapter 2 depicts it as plural, nuanced and empirically variable. This chapter pursues some further implications of this view of intimacy and focuses on issues central to an evaluation of the explanatory relevance and adequacy of the concept of the pure relationship. These issues include interpersonal power and control, self-disclosure, trust, commitment, sexual and emotional satisfaction, and the question of the 'fragility' of modern intimacy. First, let me briefly recap on the overall account of couple intimacy developed thus far.

Interpersonal control

Perhaps the major difference between the account of couple intimacy presented here and that associated with the pure relationship centres on the role played by interpersonal power, control and influence. Neither Giddens (1992) nor Beck and Beck-Gernsheim (1995) assign any importance to the influence of the interpersonal domain on intimacy, whereas it is central to the present account. 'Dynamic' ('mutually satisfying') intimacy depends, *in the main*, on benign control and influence although elements of soft manipulation and self-interest also play a role. However, partner's power and control positions remain flexible, never becoming fixed or frozen so that one partner is dominant. There are labile (and sometimes potentially volatile) alternations of power, influence and control within such relationships. However, in order for the relationship to remain stable, partners must retain a *felt sense* of control and influence over the relationship.

Mutual satisfaction is thwarted to the extent that benign control becomes displaced by 'harder' manipulation and exploitation – and this tends to go hand in hand with the emergence of relatively fixed power positions. Thus 'dynamic' (mutually satisfying) intimacy deteriorates in direct proportion to the loss of mutual benign control, as one or both partners begin to realise that they no longer have a felt sense of control and influence in the relationship. In this sense interpersonal control contributes to the confluent influences of other social domains (see Chapters 5 and 12). In direct contrast to the pure relationship, this account suggests that the combined influence of these domains generates different types of intimacy – dynamic, episodic, semi-detached, manipulative, pretence and oppressive intimacy.

Variation in couple intimacy

Modern couple intimacy is plural, complex and multidimensional and, thus, different types of intimacy are linked with variable forms of disclosure, commitment, satisfaction, trust and so on. In turn, these are associated with differences in personal strategies and styles of intimacy, conflict and communication styles and types of intimacy games. Couple intimacy is habitual, rule-guided behaviour founded on interpersonal control and influence. Mutual benign control is essential for the satisfaction of psycho-emotional needs – although discord and disharmony are never completely eliminated from even the best relationships. Relationships that rely on manipulation, dominance or exploitation repress or deny partners' rights, interests, needs or desires. Discrete clusters of relationship habits – rules, styles, skills and strategies and ploys – give rise either to energising intimacy games with their positive emotions and mutual satisfaction, or to energy-draining games, with negative emotions and damaged intimacy.

'Dynamic' intimacy contains elements from each of five energising games (whereas in semi-detached intimacy energising games are fast unravelling, while the episodic type alternates between mutual benign and 'harder' manipulative control). In dynamic intimacy energising games help satisfy psycho-emotional needs – although the partners themselves must have the requisite intimacy skills (such as empathy, emotional rapport, ability to decipher meta-messages and so on). 'Constructive conflict', in which arguments are used to solve problems, is essential, although often elements of appeasement and retreat are also present.

In energising games partners get what they want from one another by using strategies ranging from clearly defined agreements such as 'deals and pacts', the charisma of 'personal magnetism' to diffuse emotional entanglements (as in 'persuasive', 'gift' and 'deep knowledge seduction'). All require 'emotion work', that is, partners' efforts to finesse their relationship by taking one another's feelings into account. Different clusters of elements underpin the different energising games. Games of mutual seduction and altruism focus on the bond and serve to reinforce partners' unity and togetherness. Identity-affirming and empathy games focus more on individuality and an appreciation of partner's special qualities. Games of mutual support place equal emphasis on individuals and their bond by encouraging personal development at the same time as placing a high value on teamwork.

A move down through 'dynamic', to 'episodic', to 'semi-detached' intimacy may be followed by an eventual return to dynamic (or episodic) intimacy. Thus, it may be a part of what Reibstein describes as 'upward and downward spirals' (1997: 145–64) in loving relationships. 'Downward spirals' may be precipitated by 'obstacles' and 'transition points' – such as different phases of child rearing, illness, disability, the unexpected loss of a job, or partners growing apart in their interests or as a consequence of being taken for granted. Upward spirals occur when couples overcome their problems either through their own efforts or through counselling.

Alternatively, the transition from dynamic to episodic to semi-detached intimacy may signify the (gradual or sudden) dissolution of a close relationship (which may eventually end up as pretence, manipulated or oppressive intimacy). In such a case partners become more self-centred and manipulative, 'stealing' control and energy by emotional bullying and blackmail. The withdrawal of respect and courtesy undermines mutual satisfaction as much as cynical deception, and manipulation. Conflict styles which create clear winners and losers such as high-level attacks and pre-emptive strikes are common, as are low-level attacks such as nagging and whingeing.

Partners adopt intimacy styles that best fit their feelings. Someone who feels vulnerable or insecure may give away power to protect himself or herself. Even more ill-advisedly, such a person may try to 'rescue' a partner who is dangerously flawed. On the other hand, an individual may seek more power through the creation of dependency in his or her partner by employing phoney seduction, emotional blackmail or emotional terrorism. In energy-draining games the matching or mismatching of partners' need profiles is central to the emotional tenor of the games they play. In manipulative and ego-centred games partners seek to dominate the relationship. In games of attrition and emotional withholding, lack of respect for partners' special qualities is frequently expressed as active dislike and/or disapproval. Addictive and co-dependent games negate both individuality and bonding because both partners' insecurities predominate. One or both may feel threatened by the other's independence, and in a mistaken, paranoid attempt to control this, they try to tie the other into a highly oppressive relationship through constant surveillance and emotional bullying.

The issue of self-disclosure

Self-disclosure in intimate relationships is by no means the uniform and unitary phenomenon suggested in depictions of the pure relationship (Giddens 1992). For instance, although mutual self-disclosure may be at its most open and vital in dynamic intimacy, it may also be used as a gambit to get one's way, rather than as a means of opening up and getting close to one another. Also in less intense relationships or those in which intimacy is eroding, disclosure may take several forms and be used in markedly different ways. For example, although self-disclosure is rationed in episodic intimacy, it may be used selectively to reduce anxiety between partners. And while frank and open disclosure is largely absent in semi-detached intimacy, partners may make a point of public displays of pseudo-disclosure in order to present themselves as a 'normal' couple (Duncombe and Marsden 1995).

The idea that self-disclosure is much more variable and complex than assumed in Giddens' account of the pure relationship is also supported by Jamieson's review of the evidence. She suggests that 'disclosing intimacy' is 'not the dominant type in most couple relationships', and points out that expressions of practical care and support are just as important (Jamieson 1998: 157). Also, 'silent intimacy' (rather than disclosing intimacy) is effective in expressing love and care through physical presence or simple acts of loyalty.

Other acts of loving and caring may not be conveyed through 'formal' disclosure as such. In this sense, for example, sensitivity, respect, courtesy and civility are essential to mutually satisfying intimacy, but they are expressed subtly and often non-verbally and certainly not in ways normally thought of as self-disclosure. The willingness to support one another in disputes with outsiders is another example in which there is no formal or explicit disclosure, but which can be regarded as acts of loyalty that remain largely 'hidden' until revealed by an incident or chance remark. In this sense intimate knowledge of another is born out of cumulative shared experience, not through deliberate disclosure.

Finally, forms of non-disclosure must not be discounted as important components of the inner workings of close relationships. From a therapeutic point of view, Craib notes that partners often have deep emotional issues, conflicts and dilemmas that are best left undisclosed at particular points in time so as not to become destructive of intimacy. In this respect, says Craib, 'a great deal of not talking is necessary', and while 'making time to talk to a partner is clearly a good idea . . . sometimes it can be important not to talk' (Craib 1994: 130).

Trust, commitment and satisfaction

Giddens claims that in the context of the pure relationship mutual self-disclosure creates strong relations of trust and commitment, which play a huge psychological role in keeping partners together. Such disclosure is part of a freely given, psychological and emotional investment in one another and is reflected in high levels of commitment and trust. However, it is clear that in some types of intimate relationship trust and commitment are less freely given and far more 'conditional'. Even in relationships offering little in the way of emotional or sexual satisfaction there is, nevertheless, a certain amount of social and psychological support that derives from being a couple. In these cases commitment and trust are filtered through a web of pseudo-positive regard for the benefits (no matter how meagre in some cases) of being together.

Contrary to the assumptions of the pure relationship there isn't a clear-cut equation between intimacy and generic forms of commitment, trust, satisfaction or disclosure. When dynamic intimacy corrodes into episodic or semi-detached types such phenomena do not disappear altogether; rather, they evolve into hybrid forms. Commitment in particular becomes gradually emptied out of emotional content and becomes transmuted into more practical or 'conditional' forms involving psychosocial protection. In such cases partners may become preoccupied with 'sustaining a sense of intimacy', not only by repairing or shoring up troubled relationships (Jamieson 1999), but in the more positive sense of feeding the flow of benign power that may energise or re-energise them. Such strategies check any tendency for intimacy to unravel and degrade into mutual pretence, manipulation or co-dependence.

The same is true for the notion of 'satisfaction' in intimacy. In real intimacy (as opposed to the rather abstract depiction of the pure relationship) mutual satisfaction is never a static, idealised state. Rather, it is dynamically fluctuating and uncertain, albeit strictly bounded by the limits set by serious manipulation and exploitation. In this sense Craib's observations are pertinent. Craib points out that a relationship brings 'emotional satisfactions and dissatisfactions in equal measure' (1998: 114) and that the dissatisfactions will include disappointment, envy, jealousy, anger, sadness and even desperation (1994). In this sense, routine turbulences put into question the idea that a generic notion of 'satisfaction' is the sole criterion by which people judge the success or otherwise of intimate relationships.

If dissatisfactions are an in-built feature of intimacy then 'satisfaction' as a generic category cannot possibly do justice to the actual range of feelings and emotions that are central to the experience of close relationships. Similarly, satisfaction is closely linked with self-disclosure in the notion of the pure relationship. But as authors like Craib and Jamieson have pointed out, periods of non-communication (not talking to each other), or deliberate non-disclosure, are also often important. They are integral to the emotion work that may keep a relationship together (the positive meaning of sustaining a sense of intimacy) over lengthy periods of time, including accepting compromises, reconciling differences and healing emotional pain.

Intimacy, fragility and interpersonal power

An important feature of the pure relationship is its inherent fragility. For Giddens (1992) in particular, the heart of the problem lies in the increasing intensification of mutual disclosure that is part and parcel of modern intimacy. As partners (or friends) open out to each other more and more – in the service of generating trust and commitment – the self becomes exposed and vulnerable, and hence the possibilities for hurt and rejection are multiplied. Thus the fragility of intimacy is correspondingly increased. For Beck and Beck-Gernsheim (1995), the fragility is further enhanced by the strain imposed by the often opposing pulls of the two distinct labour market biographies of the partners.

While there is some truth in these depictions of the fragility of modern intimacy, neither takes into account the routine influence of interpersonal power and control and the inherent tensions it produces. Mutually satisfying intimacy is not a pure, continuous or relatively stable 'state of affairs'; it involves a labile and potentially volatile set of processes. The interpersonal dynamics of power and control mean that mutually satisfying intimacy has a fluctuating, ever-emergent nature.

The potential for disruption or dissatisfaction in such relationships means that they are always moving in and out of a balance of power, influence and control.

The labile and fluctuating nature of mutually satisfying (dynamic) intimacy stands out in relief in comparison with relationships at the other end of the scale underpinned by 'hard' manipulation, mutual oppression, or by what Miller (1995) terms 'intimate terrorism' – in which anxiety is linked to the misuse or abuse of power. In such relationships intimacy has depreciated because the flowing tensile nature of dynamic, 'open' intimacy has become constricted. Either power and control has been frozen into a skewed or lopsided arrangement, or it has evolved into mutual oppression and emotional indifference.

In this sense the fragility of modern intimacy is not simply down to the psychological vulnerability of the self in the form of the possibilities for hurt and rejection that may result from 'unrestrained' mutual self-disclosure, or even the added pressure of divergent labour market biographies. The fragility of modern intimacy stems equally from the routinely labile basis of the interpersonal control on which it rests. A seeming paradox is that it is precisely this that ensures that mutually satisfying intimacy doesn't become frozen into a settled pattern of inequality or mutually tolerated dissatisfaction.

The precarious balance of dependence and independence

A further reason for the fragility of modern intimacy concerns the balance between individual's dependence (togetherness, involvement) on the one hand and their independence (separateness, individuality) on the other. An underlying assumption of this study is that we are, in equal measure, unique, independently acting and thinking individuals *as well as* social creatures who at every turn are influenced by our social environment (Layder 1997). Such an approach opposes a rigid division between an emphasis on the importance of independence (as in versions of therapy and feminism) as against an emphasis on dependence – especially in the context of marital intimacy (Reibstein 1997). A proper understanding of intimacy must acknowledge the balance between individuality and togetherness. In this sense, genuine *inter*dependence can only properly be achieved if individuals have enough self-esteem and approval to sustain them as truly independent beings. Only then can the necessary balance of motivation and restraint for mutually satisfying intimacy be achieved.

If a person is dependent on others for his or her self-esteem or approval then their close relationship will be out of alignment. One partner's greater dependence will disrupt and skew the *inter*dependence that is required by an intimate bond because it places an unfair burden on one person to fill up the void in the other's life by constantly attending to their needs and insecurities. In the context of modern intimacy the abrogation of self-responsibility provides another source of pressure on 'the pure relationship' itself. Intimacy in the modern world must satisfy both partners' psycho-emotional needs, at the same time as it fulfils functions that were once supplied by the social community (Giddens 1992, Beck and Beck-Gernsheim 1995, Perel 2007).

Over-dependence makes intimacy impossible. Genuine intimacy requires insight into personal limitations and frailties, as well as strengths. Again a balance is required. An excessive preoccupation with either weakness or strength (egotism) will undermine mutual satisfaction. Only a mature individualism can come to terms with the 'existential aloneness' that characterises the human condition (Sartre 1966), and the consequent need to embrace self-responsibility. In this sense, taking responsibility entails being accountable for what becomes of us, what we make of ourselves, and for our thoughts and desires. But the difficulty of achieving this kind of maturity is that intimate relationships create a sense of emotional connection with others which can easily be misused as a convenient excuse to abandon self-responsibility.

And yet personal power and responsibility are essential in order for individuals to make things happen, or alter their life circumstances. Thus mature individualism in both partners pumps up the positive, energising emotions on which mutually satisfying intimacy is based. Conversely, the suppression of individuality creates an overemphasis on dependence (togetherness), leading to energy-draining habits and negative emotions. Without doubt, protection and dependence are essential components of intimacy, but they are impossible to achieve without a corresponding recognition of partners' differing needs, wishes and desires. Mutually satisfying intimacy can only emerge from a balanced focus on individuality and teamwork. In this manner a true *inter*dependence can help to steer a relationship away from over-dependence, co-dependence or selfishness.

The dangers of protective-dependent intimacy

Reibstein (1997) is, of course, right to stress the importance of protection and dependence for couple intimacy, but protection and dependence

must rest on a sound basis of self-responsibility and mature individualism. In their absence there are clear dangers in emphasising the
importance of protective-dependent intimacy. A close bond will naturally afford some protection, but this cannot be its *raison d'etre*. Only
relationships that support or enhance the self-identities of the partners
can furnish mutual satisfaction. In this sense intimacy is a vehicle for
mutual exploration, personal growth and development. If protective-
dependence is, or becomes, the *raison d'etre* of a relationship, it is
likely to inflexibly restrict expressions of individuality and, as a result,
undermine rather than enhance mutual satisfaction.

While undoubted benefits accrue from safety, protection and dependence they do not wholly obviate the need for self-responsibility.
Genuine 'safety' in intimacy can only be present when autonomous
individuals create an interdependence – an agreement to share purposes,
plans and desires in a way that does not suppress individuals' needs,
rights and interests. Using intimacy as a protective shield prevents rather
than facilitates a mutually satisfying interdependence. Furthermore, the
fragility of intimacy is increased when partners off-load responsibilities and become dependent on each other for self-esteem, approval and
emotional energy. Only when the protective aspects of intimacy are
combined with respect for individuality can mutual exploration and
personal growth take place. Much of the fragility of modern intimacy
stems from the difficulty of achieving a delicate balance between individuality and teamwork (a point not generally noted by the theorists of
the pure relationship, Giddens, Beck and Beck-Gernsheim).

Modern intimacy: Beyond the pure relationship

Modern intimacy is a more inclusive, nuanced and complex phenomenon than suggested by the pure relationship. It is more accurate
and realistic to portray it as a continuum of types (dynamic, episodic,
semi-detached, manipulative, mutual pretence and oppressive), with
their variable forms of disclosure, commitment, trust, satisfaction and
so on. Furthermore, although the theorists of the pure relationship are
right about the fragile nature of modern intimacy, they do not necessarily offer the most adequate or apposite reasons to account for
this fragility. It is true, as Giddens and Beck & Beck-Gernsheim have
observed, that modern intimacy carries a much heavier weight of expectation and responsibility than in pre-modern times, and thus to an
extent, its fragility results from the increasing exposure and vulnerability of the self and the pressure of different labour market biographies.

But these are not the only, or necessarily the most important, reasons for the fragility of modern intimacy. Equally crucial is the routine influence of interpersonal control and the inherent tensions it produces in intimate partnerships, particularly those that hinge around the struggle between dependence and independence.

12
Intimacy, Power and Social Domains

Throughout this account of modern couple intimacy I have made reference both to the role of social domains and to the different forms of power and control embedded in them. In this chapter I turn to these issues in a more explicit and extended sense. Chapters 2–11 concentrated on aspects of individual and interpersonal power as they are directly involved in close relationships. Thus it might seem that structural, collective or systemic dimensions of power merely form a somewhat unobtrusive background. Actually, this would be an illusion, and artefact of the principal analytic focus of the study. In fact, structural, systemic or collective dimensions of power play a crucial role in so far as intimate (interpersonal) relationships are formed at the centre of a maelstrom of social domain and power influences.

How do interpersonal aspects of intimacy link up with wider social organisation, and power? Acknowledging the influence of social domains requires a multidimensional view of power. That is, it must be recognised that power takes on distinct guises and forms according to the domain of social reality from which it derives. Along with the domains of 'psychobiography' and 'situated activity' (respectively referring to individual and interpersonal power), there are two other domains indicating 'social structural' or 'systemic' phenomena. These are 'social settings', which influence behaviour in an immediate sense, and 'contextual resources' – the most encompassing domain of society-wide phenomena. It is crucial to recognise that social domains are not simply 'dimensions', 'areas' or 'levels' of society. Rather, they are radically different orders of social reality that are closely intertwined through social relations of power (Layder 1997, 1998b). In this sense, intimacy is a complex amalgam of the causal influences of all four

170

domains (and the powers embedded in them), as they operate in time and space.

Contextual resources include several related elements. First, society-wide divisions of class, gender and ethnicity signify reproduced inequalities of power based on the distribution of resources and access to them. In this sense they channel access to high status positions, cultural meanings, values, ideologies and expectations (about romantic love, couple intimacy, friendship and so on). They also exert a strong influence on lifestyle choices – about fashion, food, cars and taste, for instance. The power of such structural (or systemic) factors is very different from that of subjective powers, which are continually shaped and modified during the course of situated activities (interpersonal encounters). Because structural power is likely to be entrenched, it is often resistant and slow to change. Certainly, structural power isn't easily altered by the actions of individuals – in the way that alterations in the balance of power and control often occur during encounters. Sometimes structural inequalities of power can only be transformed through collective endeavour (by protests, reforms, pressure groups and so on).

Although structural power, cultural ideas and ideologies (in this case about intimacy) shape and constrain behaviour, they don't determine it in any absolute sense. People are not ciphers, hollow puppets or plastic creations of such influences. To varying extents individuals may overcome limitations of skills and opportunities created by inequalities of class, gender and ethnicity. They are also free to reject or believe in what celebrity or lifestyle magazines say about friendship, or falling in love, as well as more traditional or institutional values and expectations about such things. In this sense people selectively draw from cultural ideas or the habitus of their origin, rather than become helplessly entrapped within their boundaries. Individuals have very different life experiences and opportunities, which equip them with unique skills and capacities. Thus, an individual's subjective powers may enable them to overcome disadvantages or resist dominant cultural influences.

Social settings and intimacy

The effects of structural power are also conditioned by the domain of 'social settings', which are socially organised locations embedding different forms of social behaviour. Intimate relationships and encounters don't float in vacuum; they occur in socially defined settings, at work, in the family, on the street, as part of a criminal subculture or as a facet of some sporting or leisure activity. Social settings provide the physical location for action – a pub, a house, an office, a bedroom, a courtroom, a factory, a hospital, a school, an airport lounge, a government bureaucracy. But they are far more than physical locales. More importantly, they are webs of social relations, positions and practices that help shape people's behaviour. For example, work organisations direct and influence the behaviour of workers, while family life and friendship networks define what is meant by parenthood, or loyalty in friendship.

Many social settings are associated with formal power structures and authority systems such as factories, offices, schools, universities, religious and military institutions and government bureaucracies. In them, appropriate behaviour is defined and controlled through relations of authority. Intimate settings like families, sexual and/or romantic partnerships and friendships are far less formally organised. Certainly, some aspects of intimate relationships are legally enforced (e.g. the Child Support Agency), to prevent certain types of exploitation. But largely, norms, expectations and values about friendship, parenthood or sexuality are learned informally through tradition, custom and practice. What it is to be a good friend or parent or lover, or what is inappropriate behaviour in these roles and relationships are more loosely defined.

Personal relationships and interpersonal power

What about personal relationships? It is best to envisage the influence of the domains working from the most 'macro lever of contextual resources, *downwards* into social settings, and *upwards* from the micro domains of psychobiography to situated activity (encounters). This imagery indicates the manner in which personal relationships influence, and are influenced by, social domains. To view the domains in a vertical plane in this manner is useful up to a point, but they are also stretched out in time and space – which is better indicated by a horizontal plane. The domains act on and through each other simultaneously and are tightly bound together through social relations of power. Personal relationships result from the combined influence of these intertwined forms of power. It follows that they cannot be understood by focusing exclusively on one domain.

In this respect, although of crucial importance for understanding some aspects of intimacy, structural inequalities in themselves (see Jamieson 1998) do not account for interpersonal variations in intimacy found in everyday practices. Structural inequalities are always conditioned by social settings, situated activity and psychobiographies. Thus the influence of class, gender, age or ethnicity on social behaviour is never direct, unmediated or straightforward. It is always subtle, complex and modified by the influences of the other domains. In a parallel manner an exclusive focus on interaction (Goffman 1983, Collins 2005) obscures the crucial conditioning influence of other domains. This would also be true for an exclusively psychological, psychoanalytic or psychotherapeutic influence (as Miller, 1995, points out). Similarly, Giddens' (1984) 'theory of structuration' (which provides the analytic background to his notion of the 'pure relationship') elides the 'emergent' aspects of interpersonal power and the mobile inequalities that are intrinsic to them. As a consequence, he over-stresses the egalitarian, democratising potential of pure relationships (Giddens 1992).

Intimate relationships are in the 'eye of the storm', the centre of multiple domain powers and their effects. Individuals draw from a range of available power and control resources in pursuing their intimacy needs and desires. Because even optimal or mutually satisfying intimacy involves at least some traces of gentle manipulation or other 'unfair' means, encounters between lovers or friends have a constantly shifting balance of power and emphasis, as individuals employ different resources, skills and ploys to elicit loving, caring responses from one another. Thus as partners or friends negotiate their relationships in everyday encounters, they draw from shifting configurations of domain resources.

For example, if personal charm or persuasive skills don't have the desired effect, there may be a shift of emphasis to gift giving (like sex, or special attention or 'understanding'). Similarly, showing appropriate empathy and disclosing one's own feelings may be effective when other skills, ploys or resources are not. Thus, in any one encounter intimates may draw from a combination of structural influences like discourses, gender or class habitus, as well as subjective powers and abilities. But the overall configuration of power and control and the emotional tenor of intimate encounters will be reshaped constantly according to the way in which the encounter unfolds as well as the unique contributions of the individuals themselves. Thus, in specific encounters the exact mix of power influences will vary in terms of a unique amalgam of domain influences. This, of course, demands a view of power as multidimensional and diverges from the idea that power takes a singular ontological form – as in Foucault's (1977, 1980) discursive practices, Habermas' (1984, 1987) systemic domination, or the ability of individual or collective actors to achieve particular ends (Weber 1964, Giddens 1984).

The need for a comprehensive approach

The importance of grasping the orchestrated effects of all social domains for understanding intimacy cannot be understated and is brought into sharp relief when we examine approaches in which the influence of one or more domains is omitted or overlooked. From this point of view, while Goffman provides us with a masterly sociological account of interpersonal behaviour, he does rather overstress the influence of what he calls 'the interaction order' (Goffman 1983). As a consequence, he neglects the equally important conditioning influence of psychobiography, while also underemphasising the role of social settings and contextual resources – although he does acknowledge the 'loosely coupled' link with institutional phenomena (see Layder 1997, 2006, for a more detailed discussion of Goffman's approach). From the point of view of domain theory, Goffman was right to highlight the relatively independent properties of the interaction order (including its importance for self-identities and the creation of meaning and so on), but he was remiss in denying, or at least understating, the conditioning effects of the other domains.

Furthermore, while Goffman did capture some important aspects of interpersonal processes, he was little concerned about the problem of power, or its multidimensional nature. Thus, he omits any consideration of subjective power deriving from psychobiographies or of systemic power (deriving from social settings and contextual resources). And while he occasionally refers to inequalities of status (and the power on which they rest), his writing doesn't include an analysis of the role of power in interpersonal relations.

Goffman shares with a number of others (including symbolic interactionists, Blumer 1969, and ethnomethodologists, Garfinkel 1967) an overemphasis on 'social practices' or inter-subjective elements – which Goffman refers to under the rubric 'the interaction order'. Numerous social constructionists Coulter (1989), Harre (1983), Shotter (1983), Potter and Wetherall (1987) share the same mistaken view of this as the exclusive explanatory domain of social reality. Instead of grasping the relatively independent effects of human psychobiographies in social life, these approaches view individuals as simple reflections (ciphers, puppets) of social forces, rules, expectations, discourses, ideologies and so on. This exclusive focus on the determining influence of social practices and inter-subjectivity offers an impoverished view of personhood and self-identity (see Layder 2007 for a critique).

In many respects these approaches share in Goffman's (1967) view that in order to understand social interaction we need a psychology 'stripped and cramped' suitable for the study of track meets, bedrooms, courtrooms and breakfast tables. As he puts it, the sociological study of such phenomena demands a focus 'on moments and their men, not men and their moments'. More recently, Collins has elaborated on Goffman's stance by suggesting that human individuals 'are transient fluxes charged up by situations' (2005: 6) whose 'uniqueness' (and every-thing else we would wish to know about them) 'is moulded in a chain of encounters across time' (2005: 5). From the domain perspective, up to a point it is true that social encounters mould individual subjectivities, self-images and behavioural dispositions. But the converse is also true. Everyone has subjective powers (varying physical and psychological abilities and attributes) that help create and reformulate interpersonal encounters. On this view, individuals and situated activities contribute *in equal measure* to the character of interpersonal relations. To grasp the real nature of intimacy we must accept that individuals are not *exclu-sively* situational creatures even though they/we spend a great deal of their/our lives in a wide variety of situations. A person has an inner life that is simultaneously lived both 'inside' and 'outside' the situated encounters in which she or he participates.

Individuals, then, help create as well as transform situated encoun-ters. An excessive emphasis on the formative influence of social rules and practices obscures the fact that a person's (psychobiographically derived) unique powers leave their stamp on situated encounters. Inti-mate relationships, for instance, are replete with examples of personal domination, manipulation, emotional blackmail as well as more sub-tle and benign 'persuasion' and 'inducement', in which subjective creativity plays a large role in interpersonal behaviour. In this sense individuals cannot be reduced to the sum of their situated encoun-ters over their lifetime. And, although Collins correctly observes that an individual's emotional energies are charged up by situations, indi-viduals also charge themselves up. Through self-talk – their own inter-nal dialogue – they create moods and emotional tones that connect with pre-existing sensitivities developed during their life experiences. Of course, encounters charge up individuals, but there is an already formed psyche (with certain levels of positive or negative energy) that rubs up against situations as they arise. In this sense a person's pre-existing energy level is either enhanced or diminished by interactive encounters.

Someone who, in general, is highly energised by personal relationships may find himself or herself emotionally spent by energy-draining games with their partner (see Chapter 8). Conversely, someone who is low in emotional energy may have it boosted by being drawn into intimacy games that are energising (Chapter 9). Clearly, there is a continuous feedback loop between the emergent dynamics of situated encounters and the psychic energies of the individuals involved in them. Of course, in reality, everything hinges on exactly *who* is involved, and in *what* circumstances. However, an adequate explanation shouldn't discount, or overlook, the influence of either the domains of psychobiography or situated activity – and thus of the contributions of the unique individuals, or emergent situational factors. One set of factors should not be reduced to the influence of the other.

While these approaches overemphasise the generative potential of interaction, Giddens, on the other hand, explicitly denies the existence – and thus the importance – of the 'extra', or distinctive, influence of an interaction order that is relatively independent of institutional forces (Giddens 1987). Giddens suggests that institutional influences enter directly into social activity through what he calls the 'duality of structure', without the 'added' input of the interaction order. In this particular sense the difference between Goffman and Giddens is that Giddens envisages a much more direct and immediate connection between wider institutional and cultural expectations and the actual behaviour of intimate partners. The link isn't complicated by the influence of the (relatively) independent interaction order. Of course, Giddens does not imply that the link is a simple mechanical or deterministic one, because in practice, active, reflexive subjects (intimate partners in this case) interpret and reshape institutional expectations. However, importantly for Giddens, interpersonal dynamics in themselves do not enable or constrain behaviour differently from institutions.

Giddens may have a point in so far as there is *a sense* in which institutional factors enter directly into behaviour. But accepting this does not require a denial of the distinctive and partly independent effects of situated activity. The interpersonal processes that underpin intimate relationships and behaviour can only be fully understood as the combined influence of different but related 'social domains'. The internal dynamics of situated activity combined with subjective and wider (structural or systemic) social factors are crucial to understanding the complexities and nuances of intimate relationships. Disregarding the influence of distinct domains of social reality on modern intimacy can only lead to simplifications and over-generalisations.

Intimacy and domain influences

Since interpersonal behaviour is at the centre of a maelstrom of domain and power influences, the vision of the individual offered here is of a 'control-seeking self set within a model of embedded domains (Layder 2004a, b, Hearn 2007). In this context the reciprocal use of benign control is central to the establishment of mutually satisfying intimacy although this is always adulterated by elements of selfishness and milder forms of manipulation. Mutual satisfaction is more decisively compromised to the extent that control and influence become more seriously manipulative and exploitative (as in emotional blackmail or psychological bullying).

However, it is important not to confuse this notion of the 'control-seeking self with what Craib (1998) describes as the ideology of the 'powerful self. This, he suggests, underlies Giddens (1991, 1992) work on self-identity and intimacy which stresses the constant questioning and reconstruction of the self as it is 'required' by the reflexive nature of modern society. Craib suggests that Giddens is entrapped in an ideology of the powerful self when, in fact, in late modernity 'the self, the individual is becoming less powerful, less able to change his or her world while being subjected to changes, often radical changes, by forces well beyond his or her control or even understanding' (Craib 1998: 2). I have some sympathy with Craib's criticism here and this is further buttressed by the inadequacy of Giddens' (1984) generic notion of human agency. On this view everyone has 'transformative capacity' or the ability to alter their circumstances as an intrinsic feature of their human agency. This seems to imply not only a powerful self – one who has transformative capacity – but also, one that is shared equally by all human beings.

By contrast, the notion of the control-seeking self implies none of these things. First, as I have stressed, individuals are defined through their differing psychobiographies, which endow them with varying levels of subjective power and control (as reflected, for example, in differing levels of self-confidence, persuasiveness or the ability to get things done). Clearly, these variable powers impact on intimacy and although people are constantly engaged in negotiations of power and control in their everyday dealings, their subjective powers are not uniform, nor do they produce uniform effects. There are as many degrees and types of success or failure in interpersonal control (Layder 2004b) as there are individuals in the world. In this sense Giddens' notion of a generic transformative capacity fails to grasp the variation in individuals' tranformative powers.

Social domains and the pure relationship

Both Giddens, and Beck and Beck-Gernsheim deny, and thus neglect (more explicitly in the case of Giddens 1987), the relatively autonomous influence of what I refer to as 'situated activity (the 'interaction order' in Goffmans terms). As a result, their respective analyses overlook the subtle, but profound effect of the emergent dynamics of inter-personal negotiations on close relationships. Both Giddens, and Beck and Beck-Gemsheim adopt theoretical positions that assume a direct (unmediated) relationship between individuals (as social agents) and institutional and cultural influences on their behaviour (in Giddens, this is accomplished via 'the duality of structure'). Such a theoretical posture elides the conditioning influence of interactional dynamics that work to create a plurality of types of intimacy, forms of disclosure, commit-ment, trust and satisfaction that characterises modern intimacy. Such variation is lost through theoretical and ontological dissolution. This is perhaps why the pure relationship seems to brook little in the way of the alternative modes of intimacy described in the body of this book.

Integral to the pure relationship is the reflexive, autonomous self, and the individualising processes of modernity. In Giddens' view self-reflexivity is intrinsically aligned with egalitarianism, emancipation and 'the radical democratisation of the personal' (1992: 182). But this stands in stark contrast to opposing interpretations that have a much less optimistic tone. Craib has forcefully criticised this optimistic view by counter-posing it with an emphasis on the importance of disappoint-ment in intimate relationships as well as the limitations on autonomy set by social constraints. Also, as Jamieson reminds us, some authors (Bellah 1985, Strathern 1992, Hochschild 1994) have interpreted the constant monitoring of the self by the self as 'part and parcel of a ram-pant self-obsessive individualism or consumerism which may threaten to destroy all intimate relationships' (Jamieson 1998: 40).

Giddens suggests that 'autonomy means the successful realisation of the reflexive project of the self – the condition of relating to others in an egalitarian way' (1992: 189). However, an undue emphasis on the autonomy of the self overlooks the intrinsically situated character of the self. This, in sum, obscures the manner in which situated activity is rela-tively independent of subjective aspects of agency as well as institutional factors. Thus again, the decisive mediating and conditioning role of the interpersonal processes that push towards plurality in modern intimacy is neglected. Moreover, in many types of intimacy the self is enmeshed in manipulation and exploitation as much as it is in benignity and egalitarianism. Much depends on the plethora of personal powers, predispositions and capacities, as well as routine interpersonal games and relationship habits, all of which exemplify the complex, nuanced and multidimensional character of modern intimacy.

Bibliography

Austin, J. (1962) *How to Do Things with Words* (Oxford: Clarendon Press).

Baron-Cohen, S. (2004) *The Essential Difference* (London: Penguin).

Baxter, J. (2005) 'How High School Girls Negotiate Leadership in Public Contexts', in Baxter (ed.), *Speaking Out: The Female Voice in Public Contexts* (Basingstoke: Palgrave Macmillan).

Beck, U. and Beck-Gernsheim, E. (1995) *The Normal Chaos of Love* (Cambridge: Polity Press).

Bellah, R. (1985) *Habits of the Heart* (Berkeley: University of California Press).

Bentall, R. (2004) *Madness Explained: Psychosis and Human Nature* (London: Penguin).

Berne, E. (1966) *Games People Play* (London: Andre Deutsch).

Bernstein, B. (1972) *Class Codes & Control*, Vol. 1 (London: Paladin).

Blumer, H. (1969) *Symbolic Interactionism: Perspectives & Methods* (Englewood Cliffs, NJ: Prentice-Hall).

Borg, J. (2004) *Persuasion: The Art of Influencing People* (Harlow: Pearson Education).

Branden, N. (1985) *Honouring the Self* (New York: Bantam).

Cameron, D. (2007) *The Myth of Mars and Venus: Do Men and Women Really Speak Different Languages?* (Oxford: Oxford University Press).

Cancian, F. (1987) *Love in America: Gender and Self-Development* (Cambridge: Cambridge University Press).

Collins, R. (2005) *Interaction Ritual Chains* (New Jersey: Princeton University Press).

Coulter, J. (1989) *Mind in Action* (Cambridge: Polity Press).

Craib, I. (1992) *Anthony Giddens* (London: Routledge).

Craib, I. (1994) *The Importance of Disappointment* (London: Routledge).

Craib, I. (1998) *Experiencing Identity* (London: Sage).

De Angelis, B. (1992) *Secrets About Men Every Woman Should Know* (London: Element).

Duncombe, J. and Marsden, D. (1995) 'Can Men Love? Reading Staging and Resisting the Romance', in L. Pearce and J. Stacey (eds), *Romance Revisited* (London: Lawrence Wishart), pp. 238–50.

Forward, S. and Frazier, D. (1998) *Emotional Blackmail* (London: Bantam).

Foucault, M. (1977) *Discipline & Punish* (London: Allen Lane).

Foucault, M. (1980) *A History of Sexuality* (New York: Vintage).

Fromm, E. (1971) *The Art of Loving* (London: Allen & Unwin).

Garfinkel, H. (1967) *Studies in Ethnomethodology* (Englewood Cliffs: Prentice-Hall).

Giddens, A. (1984) *The Constitution of Society* (Cambridge: Polity Press).

Giddens, A. (1987) *Social Theory & Modern Sociology* (Stanford: Stanford University Press).

Giddens, A. (1991) *Modernity and Self Identity* (Cambridge: Polity Press).

Giddens, A. (1992) *The Transformation of Intimacy* (Cambridge: Polity Press).

Gilbert, P. (1992) *Depression: The Evolution of Powerlessness* (Hove: Lawrence Erlbaum).

Goffman, E. (1967) *Interaction Ritual* (New York: Anchor).

Goffman, E. (1971) *The Presentation of Self in Everyday Life* (Harmondsworth: Penguin).

Goffman, E. (1983) 'The Interaction Order', *American Sociological Review*, 48: 1–17.

Goldman, A. (1988) *The Lives of John Lennon* (London: Bantam).

Goleman, D. (1996) *Emotional Intelligence* (London: Bloomsbury).

Goodwin, M. (2006) *The Hidden Life of Girls: Games of Stance, Status and Exclusion* (Maiden, MA: Blackwell).

Gottman, J. (2006) 'Connect and Respect', *Psychologies*, February: 90–1.

Gray, J. (1992) *Men Are from Mars, Women Are from Venus* (New York: Harper Collins).

Habermas, J. (1984) *The Theory of Communicative Action Vol. 1: Reason and the Rationalisation of Society* (Cambridge: Polity Press).

Habermas, J. (1987) *The Theory of Communicative Action Vol. 2: The Critique of Functionalist Reason* (Cambridge: Polity Press).

Harre, R. (1983) *Personal Being: A Theory for Individual Psychology* (Oxford: Blackwell).

Hearn, J. (2007) 'National Identity: Banal, Personal and Embedded', *Nations and Nationalism*, 13(4) July.

Hochschild, A. (1983) *The Managed Heart* (Berkeley, CA: University of California Press).

Hochschild, A. (1994) 'The Commercial Spirit of Intimate Life and the Abduction of Feminism: Signs from Women's Advice Books', *Theory, Culture and Society*, 11: 1–24.

Holmes, J. (2006) *Gendered Talk in the Workplace* (Oxford: Blackwell).

Horley, S. (2000) *The Charm Syndrome* (London: Refuge).

Hyde, J. (2005) 'The Gender Similarities Hypothesis', *American Psychologist*, 60(6): 581–92.

Jamieson, L. (1998) *Intimacy: Personal Relationships in Modern Societies* (Cambridge: Polity Press).

Jamieson, L. (1999) 'Intimacy Transformed? A Critical Look at the Pure Relationship', *Sociology*, 33(3): 477–94.

Jeffers, S. (1987) *Feel the Fear and Do it Anyway* (London: Arrow).

Jenkins, R. (1994) 'Rethinking Ethnicity: Identity, Categorization and Power', *Ethnic and Racial Studies* 17(2): 197–223.

Kaspersen, L. (2000) *Anthony Giddens: An Introduction to a Social Theorist* (Oxford: Blackwell).

Laing, R. (1969) *The Divided Self* (Harmondsworth: Penguin).

Layder, D. (1997) *Modern Social Theory: Key Debates & New Directions* (London: University College London Press/Taylor & Francis).

Layder, D. (1998) 'The Reality of Social Domains: Implications for Theory & Method' in T. May and M. Williams (eds), *Knowing the Social World* (Buckingham: Open University Press).

Layder, D. (2004a) *Social and Personal Identity: Understanding Yourself* (London: Sage).

Layder, D. (2004b) *Emotion in Social Life: The Lost Heart of Society* (London: Sage).

Layder, D. (2006) *Understanding Social Theory*, 2nd Edition (London: Sage).

182 *Bibliography*

Layder, D. (2007) 'Self-Identity and Personhood in Social Analysis: The Inadequacies of Postmodernism and Social Constructionism', in J. Powell and T. Owen (eds), *Reconstructing Postmodernism: Critical Debates* (New York: Nova Science).
Lennon, C. (2005) *John* (London: Hodder & Stoughton).
Lukes, S. (2005) *Power: A Radical View*, 2nd edition (Basingstoke: Palgrave Macmillan).
Malone, M. (1997) *Worlds of Talk: The Presentation of Self in Everyday Conversation* (Cambridge: Polity Press).
Maltz, D. and Borker, R. (1983) 'A Cultural Approach to Male-Female Miscommunication', in J. Gumperz (ed.), *Language and Social Identity* (New York: Cambridge University Press).
Marshall, A. (2006) *I Love You But I'm Not in Love With You* (London: Bloomsbury).
Maslow, A. (1999) *Towards a Psychology of Being*, 3rd edition (New York: Wiley).
Miller, M. (1995) *Intimate Terrorism: The Crisis of Love in an Age of Disillusion* (New York: Norton).
Moir, A. and Moir, B. (1999) *Why Men Don't Iron* (New York: Citadel).
Norwood, R. (2004) *Women Who Love Too Much* (London: Arrow).
Pease, A and Pease, B. (2002) *Why Men Lie and Women Cry* (London: Orion).
Peele, S. and Brodsky, A. (1974) *Love and Addiction* (London: Abacus).
Perel, E. (2007) *Mating in Captivity: Sex Lies and Domestic Bliss* (London: Hodder and Stoughton).
Person, E. (1990) *Love and Fateful Encounters* (London: Bloomsbury).
Potter, J. and Wetherall, M. (1987) *Discourse and Social Psychology: Beyond Attitudes and Behaviour* (London: Sage).
Quilliam, S. (2001) *Stop Arguing, Start Talking* (London: Vermillion).
Rawls, A. (1987) 'The Interaction Order *Sui Generis*: Goffman's Contribution to Social Theory', *Sociological Theory*, 5: 136–49.
Redfield, J. and Adrienne, C. (1995) *The Celestine Prophecy: An Experiential Guide* (London: Bantam).
Reibstein, J. (1997) *Love Life: How to Make Your Relationship Work* (London: Fourth Estate).
Reid-Thomas, H. (1993) 'The Use and Interpretation by Men and Women of Minimal Responses in Informal Conversation', MLitt thesis, Strathclyde University.
Rogers, C. (1998) *On Becoming a Person: A Therapists View of Psychotherapy* (London: Constable).
Sartre, J.-P. (1966)*Being and Nothingness* (New York: Simon and Schuster).
Scheff, T. (1966) *Being Mentally Ill* (Chicago: Aldine).
Scheff, T. (1990) *Microsociology: Discourse, Emotion and Social Structure* (Chicago: University of Chicago Press).
Seaman, F. (1991) *John Lennon: Living on Borrowed Time* (London: Xanadu Publications).
Shotter, J. (1983) *Conversational Realities* (London: Sage).
Smith, D. (1988) *The Everyday World as Problematic* (Milton Keynes: Open University Press).
Stewart, S. (1998) *Shattered Dreams* (London: Mainstream).
Strathern, M. (1992) *After Nature: English Kinship in the late Twentieth Century* (Cambridge: Cambridge University Press).
Tannen, D. (1992) *You Just Don't Understand* (London: Virago).

Tannen, D. (2002) *I Only Say This because I Love You* (London: Virago).

Templar, R. (2006) *The Rules of Life* (Harlow: Pearson Educational).

The Times (2007) *Times*, 2 July, 11: 6.

Tolle, E. (2005) *A New Earth* (London: Penguin).

Vaitkus, S. (1991) *How is Society Possible?* (Dordrecht: Kluwer Academic).

Weber, M. (1964) *The Theory of Social and Economic Organization* (New York: Free Press).

Weinstein, E. and Deutschberger, P. (1963) 'Some Dimensions of Altercasting', *Sociometry*, 26: 454–66.

Index

Note: Locators in **bold** type indicate figures, those in *italics* indicate tables.